Stickin' To, Watchin' Over, and Gettin' With

Howard C. Stevenson
Gwendolyn Davis
Saburah Abdul-Kabir

Stickin' To, Watchin' Over, and Gettin' With

An African American Parent's Guide to Discipline

JOSSEY-BASS
A Wiley Company
www.josseybass.com

JOSSEY-BASS
A Wiley Company
989 Market Street
San Francisco, CA 94103-1741

www.josseybass.com

Jossey-Bass books and products are available through most bookstores. To contact Jossey-Bass directly, call (888) 378-2537, fax to (800) 605-2665, or visit our website at www.josseybass.com.

Substantial discounts on bulk quantities of Jossey-Bass books are available to corporations, professional associations, and other organizations. For details and discount information, contact the special sales department at Jossey-Bass.

We at Jossey-Bass strive to use the most environmentally sensitive paper stocks available to us. Our publications are printed on acid-free recycled stock whenever possible, and our paper always meets or exceeds minimum GPO and EPA requirements.

Library of Congress Cataloging-in-Publication Data

Stevenson, Howard C., date.
   Stickin' to, watchin' over, and gettin' with: an African American parent's guide to discipline / Howard C. Stevenson, Gwendolyn Davis, Saburah Abdul-Kabir.—1st ed.
      p. cm.
   ISBN 0-7879-5702-X
   1. Discipline of children—United States. 2. African American children. I. Davis, Gwendolyn, date. II. Abdul-Kabir, Saburah, date. III. Title.
HQ770.4 .S748 2001
649'.64—dc21   2001003465

FIRST EDITION
PB Printing   10 9 8 7 6 5 4 3 2 1

Contents

In memory of
Alice Golden Stevenson
and
Frances Myers Davis

Preface

When we decided to write a book on African American discipline many years ago, we were struggling with where to start. There are so many controversies about what are the "right" and "wrong" discipline strategies. We stopped and started, over and over again, because we weren't sure who the audience should be or how we should package the knowledge we'd gained over two decades.

We wondered about the controversies over different discipline strategies across cultural groups that social workers, psychologists, teachers, and families discussed. All three of us had worked intensively as counselors, researchers, and teachers with families and parents from a variety of racial backgrounds and had confronted the issue of whether it is appropriate to spank children. But because professionals and researchers often took an "either-or," right or wrong position, the task seemed burdensome. We often struggled with White colleagues who were sensitive to the dilemmas of parenting in general but very fearful of addressing the racial and cultural dynamics. In our opinion the day-to-day life dilemmas, racism pressures, and compromises that parents go through were missing from these controversies.

We were worried about how the academic community would receive a book that focused solely on African American discipline. We were worried that some might not consider it useful to talk so specifically about discipline without evidence for each and every statement of advice. We were also worried that writing such a book might only bring, to a larger public, negative assumptions about "what Black people do" and might give less caring professionals ammunition to denigrate the behaviors of Black parenting. This is the "don't air dirty laundry" fear.

But then we remembered that in the common literature we rarely found the voice of the families we had worked with (and who had worked with us) over the years. What many Black families experience, believe, and voice in a racially charged context is often missing from the readings on Black families. At some point we realized that we needed to focus not on how folks might distort our message but on who our audience was. So we chose to focus on the parents. This book is for them.

In the debate over whether spanking is appropriate, the issue of the well-being of Black children and families has been lost. In our experience those who have supported physical discipline have justified it on the grounds that children today, living in a very crazy world, are unruly and need correction and accountability. Those who reject physical discipline reject any support for it, considering it detrimental to the mental and physical health of children under any circumstances. These are all protective reasons, but they belittle the challenging task of parenting and narrow the complexity of what it means to raise a respectful child of color.

In our opinion, in order to help children to grow up emotionally strong and healthy, it is useful to understand the life conditions, family and cultural history, and personal psychological struggles of parents who choose to use all forms of discipline. Why? We think the debate is about staying distant from the daily lives of parents who live different and difficult lives. Racism is evident in the actions of critics who, rather than trying to understand family structures and culturally different behaviors, make policies that attack those structures and behaviors. The effective discipline of children is an issue for every ethnic and racial group in America. While research suggests that there is more of a tendency to engage in physical discipline in lower-income families than in other families, because of the stress of poverty, this and other explanations get lost in the debate over physical discipline. And yes, there are other forms of discipline.

We focus on Black parents specifically because we think they get identified in this debate as more likely to use physical discipline than any other group. We believe the breadth and depth of the cultural strengths and strategies of Black culture and behavior get lost in the debate. At the same time, we want to reconnect Black parents to their historical, cultural, and spiritual roots to aid in their struggles to discipline their children.

We want to bring the focus of discipline back to the cultural life experiences of parents and children of African American descent. One way to do this is to identify why parents would use physical discipline. Another way is to understand the reasons behind the use of any form of discipline and provide alternative rationales. Still another way is to avoid narrowing the discipline debate to simply physical strategies. In our view cultural style matters, and so throughout the book, we have chosen various styles to broaden the definition of discipline and to present our suggestions to African American and biracial parents with varied life experiences.

We abhor and reject any attempts by social workers, psychologists, or helpers to give blanket edicts about how to raise a Black child, without any relationship with or knowledge of Black folk, history, and varied cultural experiences. These "social critics" are not helpful to the cause of Black youth development in America simply because they have no intimate experience with the challenges of such a task. Black children need a variety of strategies to manage what is, at best, a racially ambivalent society. Too often we have seen helpers view Black families from a distance and out of fear and stereotypes make blanket statements or take faulty steps "for the sake of the child." Yet they have spent little time "getting in the mix" of why Black parents do what they do, nor do they care.

Fear of the racial complexities of child rearing on the part of professionals, or the refusal to discuss this fear, is a clear indication that those professionals are severely limited in their ability to offer parenting advice to Black families. For us the discipline of Black youth requires parents to provide love, supervision, and accountability while keeping their eyes wide open to the racial and gender oppression in the air. We call these three discipline ingredients *affection, protection,* and *correction.* To depend on any one of these without the other two is not discipline in our view. The debate about physical discipline usually misses the boat on all three.

We wrote this book to Black parents because we feel researchers and helpers need to learn more about how to talk directly to families who are not researchers and professionals. We hope that many parents with children of African American descent will read this book and feel that we've captured many of their cultural experiences. It is also our hope that researchers and professionals will learn from parents—by listening to the conversations we are having with them—rather than the other way around.

Although we will continue to write research articles, talking to Black parents directly about discipline is one way to help us to keep our commitments to the many folks who have taught us not to forget our roots. To forget where you came from, who you grew up with, or how you came to be is like slowly dying from malnutrition. We chose life. This book is one step in that direction.

Howard is a father of one, Saburah, a mother of six, and Gwendolyn, the youngest of fourteen siblings. A lot of the suggestions in this book come from our own family experiences and from our many years of experience with Black families, as clinicians, researchers, and natural neighborhood healers. We believe we bring different angles to the topic of discipline. So, in a sense, we wrote this book for ourselves as well as for anyone else.

Acknowledgments

First, we want to thank the Creator, God Almighty, for stickin' to, watchin' over, and gettin' with us long before, during, and after this book. Special thanks go to our parents, family, brothers, and sisters, who raised us and shaped us the best way they knew how. Thanks to Dad, Howard Sr., who was always present for every event, supporting and encouraging us. Thanks to Mom, who was not shy in showing us affection every day of our lives but who, like a hawk, would rip the heart out of anyone who tried to mess with our cultural spirits and souls. We wish to thank all the folks who raised us in the neighborhoods we grew up in. We are grateful to the many visible and invisible "aunts and uncles" and "moms and dads" from Sunday school to high school who took the time to challenge us, scold us, embrace us, and watch us when we played, when we fell, and even when we left home. Without those many eyes, the larger village of caring adults, we would not be able to see deeply into ourselves. Thanks to Margaret Spencer, who as a colleague and friend has provided affection, protection, and correction and reminded us to be prepared daily for the world we are living in. Finally, special thanks to our children, Bryan, Sahir, Sana, Safwan, Siddique, Safiyah, and Sabriyah for teaching us not to forget what it means to be human.

July 2001
Philadelphia, Pennsylvania

HOWARD C. STEVENSON
GWENDOLYN DAVIS
SABURAH ABDUL-KABIR

Introduction

The lion's story will never be known as long as the
hunter is the one to tell it.

                              African proverb

Derek and Renee, angry and ready to pounce, had just sent their twelve-
year-old to his room for being disobedient. They found out that Jamal
was with his friends throwing rocks at an abandoned house some blocks
away and breaking its windows.

"Boy, you know you don't belong over there! What did we tell you?"
they say.

"What's the big deal?" he replies. "All my friends go over there and
do stuff!"

Derek and Renee realize that the local authorities or other folks who
see Black boys as naturally hostile and disobedient may misinterpret the
stone throwing of Jamal and his homies. They both believe that he will get
no second chances to explain his behavior.

"What if the police come by, as they always do, looking to catch you
looking like you're doing something wrong, huh?" Renee reminds him. "Do
you think the police are going to care that all your friends are with you doing
the same thing? They'll charge you with trespassing or property destruction
or just make something up because you're Black and up to no good."

These worried parents tell their son that some other kids may be able
to get away with throwing rocks at buildings but they don't want him to
do it because someone may think he is a troublemaker or worse.

1

"This perception is not right, but it still happens, and we want you to be ready for it."

They hug Jamal and tell him they love him but everybody doesn't know him the way they know him. Other people won't care about him or believe that he wants to be a lawyer one day.

"Obedience to your parents now may save your life later. Do you hear us, Jamal?" He nods with some understanding of what his parents are talking about. He accepts "being grounded" for two days during which he cannot go out with his friends. This is meant to remind him that he will be held accountable for disobeying his parents' rules. Derek and Renee breathe a sigh of relief but pray aloud to God that Jamal will one day understand what all of this means, the way they do.

❧

The hardest job in America today is raising children—especially African American children. It's not because Black children are more problematic than others. It's because the window of opportunity, the avenue of prosperity, and the benefit of the doubt are so narrow and rare that Black parents sweat every day over whether their children will survive through these many obstacles and come home safe and well. So given that America has a long history of rejecting the strengths and talents of African Americans, parenting an African American child holds unique and additional burdens.

This is a book about how parents can help their children fulfill every opportunity, achieve prosperity, and get past that societal hostility and doubt to enjoy a fair measure of safety and security. The path we're recommending to parents for achieving these goals, as you'll see, is discipline. We believe that using discipline is the most effective way parents can help children do the best they can. And we've written a whole book about this because we realize that discipline is a controversial topic with a lot of different approaches.

In this book we define the word *discipline* broadly. It is not uncommon in the Black community to hear parents speak about discipline in terms of the biblical phrase "Spare the rod and spoil the child." Usually, this phrase creates images of spanking children to correct them before they grow up to be rude and hated adults. It also conjures up fears in parents that friends and relatives will critique their parenting ability for not managing their embarrassing children. "Correction, correction, correction" is the conventional meaning of this phrase for most people.

This quote actually comes from a verse in Proverbs (13:24) that says, "He who spares his rod hates his son, But he who loves him seeks him diligently with discipline." Because so many of us in the Black community refer to the "spare and spoil" phrase, we must address it directly.

If you look up the definition of the Hebrew word for *rod*, you learn that it's not meant simply as an instrument. It is also meant to represent a group of people, or a "village." It is translated as *staff* (as in a staff for chastisement), *tribe* or *branch* (of a family), and *race* (as in a race of people). Interesting. This suggests that the word *rod* refers not only to physical discipline but also to the wisdom and caring of the tribe, the family, the community, the race. That is, it also refers to the role that shepherding and community play in the disciplining of children. So the obvious question is whether a parent should use a whole group of people to discipline a child. Our answer would be yes.

The many images that parents have of what discipline means rarely include the use of trusted family and friends. We often take a very rugged, individualistic "Marlboro Man" mentality when it comes to parenting: "A real parent knows how to handle his or her kids!" or "*Real* parents don't need any help" or "If I was a real parent, I would be able to get my kid to behave all by myself." The truth of the matter is that children respond differently to different people. So by investing in the relationships of other caring and trustworthy adults to aid in your parenting role, you increase the chances that your child will respond positively and learn why positive social interaction is so important. You also add to your child's development as a person who can live in healthy relationships with many different kinds of people.

Moreover, "seeks him diligently" means that a committed relationship must exist between the parent and the child with consistent fervor. Now, that changes the general picture most people have of discipline as just being about spanking. We believe it is impossible to discipline effectively without relationship. Furthermore, the word *discipline* in Hebrew, *chanak*, actually means "to teach." Teaching. Shepherding. Community. Village. Therefore not only must parents work hard to engage in meaningful discipline, but they can do it better if they live within a village of supportive teachers.

So a better way of understanding these sacred words could actually be: "Parents who don't provide the wisdom of the family, the tribe, and the race deprive their children; but the parent who loves the children will invite and accept consistent and fervent teaching from the whole community."

Consequently, we believe that discipline is more than spanking or the fear of punishment. We see discipline as a shepherding process of praise and accountability, along with a series of loving acts that are best accomplished within a community of committed teaching relationships. Given this broader view of discipline, what are the key ingredients?

THREE KEY INGREDIENTS OF EFFECTIVE DISCIPLINE

In our view raising Black children takes high levels of three key ingredients: affection, protection, and correction.

It takes lots of courage and determination to nurture, supervise, and discipline children while overcoming the everyday, ever so subtle, on-the-television, in-the-school, self-esteem-challenging, and life-threatening racial hostility. It takes cultural fortitude to face the unpredictability of racial intolerance. But most of all, it takes a village of relationships with young and old who hold culturally relevant wisdom to conquer long-standing and systematic discrimination.

This book is about how "discipline" builds relationships full of affection, protection, and correction strategies. And discipline is an essential component in the healthy development of African American children, family, and community.

Discipline works best when children trust their parents. To separate discipline from trust is like having a house with no heat in the wintertime. Even though you have a roof over your head, you may still freeze to death. Parents who instill fear but not trust often build a house made of mortar but fail to heat the people in it. And then we wonder why it's cold in the house or why our children feel like they're left out in the cold.

Children do not usually separate caring from correction. They expect that love will be attached to whatever parents do. Therefore until we understand the key ingredients to parenting, we'll always struggle to understand why our children are sometimes confused about what we mean. We believe in these three key ingredients of good discipline, but all of them center around the theme of love. So let's take a closer look.

Three Ingredients of Effective Discipline in the Black Community

1. *Stickin' To*—unconditional love and support (affection)
2. *Watchin' Over*—loving supervision (protection)
3. *Gettin' With*—loving confrontation and accountability (correction)

Stickin' To

୶

The pot will smell of what is put into it.

୶

The first ingredient of effective discipline is *Stickin' To*, which means that discipline starts with unconditional love, including plenty of hugs and kisses. *Unconditional* means just that—"I love you without conditions in spite of your mistakes." It means loving our kids, ourselves, our family, and our Creator, in good times and bad times. So when we commit to unconditional love for our children, we should expect them to change the world.

A wonderful African proverb expresses this ingredient: "The pot will smell of what is put into it." If we have that in-your-face, show-up-at-your-school, watch-your-activities, listen-to-your-stories, hug-you-lots, kiss-you-much, got-your-back kind of touchy-feely love, our children will respond accordingly. If we put love into our children, we will get love back, and the world will get it back too.

Janice Ferebee, a social worker, makes a valuable point in her book *Got It Goin' On: Fitness and Fashion with Funk* when she states, "Speak life to our children because they will become what you tell them" (p. 1). Stickin' To is about building emotional caring in our children. It involves direct touch and love you can feel and see.

We know what happens to children who are not touched or acknowledged. When this country supported the large-scale housing of orphans, one of the tragic findings of this plan was that many became listless and depressed because they received so little physical contact. The same phenomenon can be seen in some of today's youth who show harshness toward the pain of others. It's primarily because they have very few examples of, and very little experience with, the power and hope of unconditional love from the people they care about the most.

Unconditional love means loving your child whether or not

1. He gets A's or D's
2. She goes to Penn State or the state penitentiary
3. She becomes famous or unknown
4. He becomes a doctor or an artist
5. He is gay or straight

It goes without saying that love and affection are key to the survival of African American youth. What makes it worth repeating is the fact that too many Black youth are still not sure if they are loved. By affection, or Stickin' To, we mean physical demonstrations of love as well as emotional connections. We also feel that whether you are ten days, ten months, ten years, or ten decades old, you'll always need both physical and emotional affirmation of your existence and demonstration that someone loves you. When we talk about affection, or Stickin' To, we mean in a physically and emotionally unrestrained way, as if to say, "Come hell or high water, you belong to me, and I will let you know it until the day you die!"

Why is it that we start out giving our little ones all the kisses and hugs and physical goodies but then slowly reduce this as they grow up into adolescence and adulthood? When we speak to parents, we always try to remind them to grab and hug their teenagers as much as their infants—especially if they resist. Why? Because African American youth are most often pictured as hostile, sex-ridden, aggressive, and unlovable predators. And their parents aren't usually held in high regard either. Therefore we must undermine this image for our children (who are easily swayed by such images), so they will not adopt an oppositional identity just to be somebody. Before and while our youth internalize these images, we must embrace them like babies and demonstrate our affection, from the cradle to the grave. If they get mad at us for hugging them too much, let it become a story they tell their friends.

Watchin' Over

One tree receiving all the wind breaks.

The second ingredient to effective discipline is *Watchin' Over*. Watchin' Over means a number of other functions. It means watching what your children do, hearing what they say, and noticing what they don't say. It means watching their facial expressions and reading their feelings. It helps us understand who our children are and what their needs are. Parents are the first teachers, so we don't want to give up on that job just because our children go to school. Watchin' Over means you know your children well enough to know if someone is talking about them accurately or not. We need to watch over our children because we can protect them better than anyone else. Protection of African American children is essential to their future outcomes. When we survey national health statistics, we find that Black children rank highest on lists of preventable social ills compared with any other children in the world. From violence to poverty to hatred, Black children, in greater percentages, must endure enormous emotional and physical onslaughts. Community and adult supervision is required if we expect them to reach the age of eighteen, let alone become adults.

We have heard so many statistics about the victimization of African American children. Some suggest that it would be easier for starving children in Bangladesh to make it to the age of eighteen than for African American children who are exposed to violence in their neighborhoods and racism in their lives. Homicide still ranks as the primary cause of death for Black males between the ages of sixteen and thirty-two. Injury from fighting, handguns, and other weapons is a larger threat than homicide to the health of Black youth. Who wants to go through needless funeral after needless funeral, watching children die because others didn't like the way the children looked at them? Unfortunately, these and other aggressive reactions often stem from the lack of protection that children and adults feel. Aggression is an exaggerated and often self-destructive way to protect oneself. As parents, we have to help our youth find a better way.

The prison, or "corrections," industry is one of the fastest growing businesses in America, and prisons are growing primarily in high-unemployment residential settings of predominantly White homes and families. In more ways than one, the building of prisons and the excessive jailing of "Black youth" has economic benefits for many people out of work. The word *corrections* is a misnomer given the ways in which we lock young people up and fail to provide even minimal rehabilitation opportunities. Watchin' Over means facing the sad reality that Black children just can't make mistakes and expect society to respond with forgiveness or unconditional love or even a commitment to get at the truth. Unfortunately, whereas many (not all) White children can make mistakes their whole lives and still be seen as "good people," the window of opportunity for Black children is open only a crack. One mistake may be all our children get.

Effective discipline requires supervision not only by parents but family members, neighbors, and the Creator as well. Watchin' Over implies that Black children are scapegoats in our society and need Black communities and families to protect them. While the world is using Black youth as target practice for its hostility and insecurity, our job as parents is to stand in front of them and protect them from this psychological violence. It is violent to view a child as a man when he is only ten. It is violent to assume that young Black people are going to steal from or harm you just because you see this happening all the time on TV and in the movies. And it can lead to violence when we don't challenge teachers and police when they believe our children are naturally "criminal."

Our children need protection from a violent society that shoots first and asks questions later. Only we can protect them with this special keen understanding of these "peculiar" American racial politics. To expect any societal institution or its employees to understand this is akin to expecting money to fall from the sky. You can wait for it, but you're sure to be standing there for a really long time.

Unconditional protection means

---

1. Learning what children are expected to do and know at different ages (from birth to age forty) and encouraging growth when it is the right time
2. Building relationships with caring, wise family and

friends and inviting them to help you in watching, loving, and correcting your child

3. Understanding what racism is and how it will have short- and long-term psychological effects on the health and achievement of Black youth

4. Understanding how others in society may view your child of color

5. Learning to prepare your child to manage the racial hostility he or she will face when you are not around

Reaching a day when "All men are created equal" is still possible. But parents of African American children must be vigilant until that day is not just an ideal in the minds of dead White men but also real in the minds of you and me. Until that day comes, Watchin' Over Black youth will be a daily necessity. One parent cannot expect to watch his or her child twenty-four hours a day, but the job gets easier if you have four eyes instead of two, or many eyes instead of just a few.

Howard Stevenson tells a story of how fearful he was of doing anything wrong while growing up:

I had as many thoughts about doing the "wrong thing" as the next guy. So did many of my friends and siblings. The problem was that we were deathly afraid of all the other people in the world who could catch us doing all those "wrong things." Whenever I would consider smoking or drinking or disobeying, all I could see was my church or father walking right in on me at the moment the bottle touched my mouth or the cigarette was lit. The feeling that the whole church was watching was enough to make me think two or three times before making certain "bad" decisions. What fueled these images that "my people" would walk in on me doing the wrong thing was that I grew up in a community of relationships where folks told my parents what they saw me doing, right or wrong, any time of the day.

⁂

What we want parents to consider is that protecting Black youth is a lifelong process given the racial and gender hostilities in our society. Knowing and preparing for these hostilities actually decreases paranoia and increases safety because not only can parents know what to do when racial identity is challenged but children can know what to do. And if children carry the village's wise decisions (which they learn from their relationships with wise villagers) in their head, it's the next best thing to having someone watching them twenty-four hours a day, seven days a week.

Gettin' With

∾

A child without correction is like a river without a bank.

∾

The third ingredient of healthy Black parenting involves *Gettin' With*, which means face-to-face, up-close involvement that includes correction and holding children and youth accountable for their behaviors but without breaking their spirit. By *correction*, we mean the variety of ways in which parents and their larger networks of relationships can remind children to make the best choices about their lives.

Decision making does not come from one strategy alone. Gettin' With involves recognizing that the world will view Blacks' temper tantrums as more dangerous than Whites' temper tantrums. It means facing the fact that if Black children are caught doing wrong, their punishment may be greater than for similar crimes committed by White children. A more tragic reality is that many Black youth are falsely accused of crimes simply because they are Black. Using calculations of data from the U.S. Office of Juvenile Justice and Delinquency Prevention, Marion Wright Edelman of the Children's Defense Fund reports that not only are Black youth receiving more severe and lengthy punishments than White males who are committing the same offenses, but they are overrepresented at every level of the juvenile justice system, making up 70 percent of the total population (Edelman, 2000). The perception of Black youth as inherently criminal fuels this tragedy.

Gettin' With is a necessary step not only for teaching Black children right from wrong but for explaining how the rest of the world sees them. Often African American parents have considered the racism of the world as a reason why they have to be "tough" on their children. The justification is "It is better that I be hard on you now so that the world does not have to be hard on you later." Another justification is "Maybe that White kid over there can act like a park ape in the supermarket, but you can't because they might just take you to jail." These statements are rooted in the African proverb "He who is not chastised by his parents is chastised by his ill-wisher." This is well meaning except if the chastisement is not buttressed by a committed relationship or a caring spirit. If these justifications are not surrounded by love, then they represent punishment, not the loving and shepherding support of discipline and accountability.

For us there is a big difference between punishment and accountability. Jails and prisons are places of punishment. Punishment represents a very judgmental, distant, noncaring reality that is grounded in retribution. Punishment can raise the ire of the individual if the consequences rank greater than the crime, if it is without a relationship, and if it encourages a diffusion of responsibility. Unfortunately, with punishment and no rehabilitation, eventually all you get is a hardened soul that is insensitive to the experiences and feelings of others.

African American parents have to apply accountability instead of punishment. Accountability is a refined type of discipline that reflects consistent closeness and caring, along with a sense of commitment, acceptance of responsibility, a balanced doling out of consequences, and an honoring of the community and Creator as the highest authority. It means that parents have to be knowledgeable about the behaviors of children in order to hold them accountable. It means that children can hold parents accountable too.

We believe that when parents apply punishment instead of accountability strategies, unnecessary anger and hostility will develop in children. And there is an old Black community saying: "What goes around comes around." That extra anger and hostility have to go somewhere, and they often return to drain the emotional resources of the child when he or she is faced with similar life difficulties.

Punishment Versus Accountability

Punishment	Accountability
1. Retribution is the focus.	1. Restoration is the focus.
2. Suffering is greater than learning.	2. Learning is greater than suffering.
3. Relationship is unnecessary.	3. Relationship is essential.
4. Consequences are managed alone.	4. Consequences are managed within community.
5. Society is the higher authority.	5. Community and Creator are the higher authority.

With correction children can learn about the world and themselves. So we envision a parental correction system that involves many people, all of whom have been given permission to hold children accountable for their behaviors. "Many people" can include teachers, relatives, neighbors (who live close and far), older peers, trusted friends, and siblings. And we are not talking about the gossipy, tattletale type of correction but the you-are-a-part-of-me type of accountability.

Later in the book we'll be showing you some ideas and guidelines for specific ways to provide accountability and discipline for your children, organized according to how old they are. For now, though, keep in mind that there are a broad variety of ideas and family styles, all of which can work for you, so long as you remember that "it takes a village."

Meanwhile, as long as our discipline includes the overall ingredients of Stickin' To, Watchin' Over, and Gettin' With, our children will not only be able to navigate the asteroid-filled journey of Black childhood and adolescence, but they will be able to appreciate themselves in the process. If you are communicating your helplessness to your child through your correction strategies, you are probably not being effective. Furthermore, if children are not reading from you that you love them, you are also not being effective. If you do not take care of yourself physically or emotionally, you most likely are not being effective. And finally, if you are continually using the same strategy without thought as to why, you just might be having a pretty hard time.

WHY DO WE NEED A SPECIAL BOOK ON DISCIPLINE FOR AFRICAN AMERICAN PARENTS?

Black parents have a unique challenge in this society. Other ethnicities and cultural groups in the United States have their issues, but frankly we don't think any community has quite the special challenges that we face. How we treat our children today is not only a statement about our future but a reflection of our past experiences as children and as a people who have endured enormous hardships. Our children depend on us to protect, affect, and correct them. We will show how the cultural family rituals, traditions, proverbs, and life experiences of African Americans can be used to advise parents to raise healthy, wealthy, and wise children. This book will help African American parents learn how to integrate affection, protection, and correction strategies into their parenting from the moment their children are born into this world.

Why do we need a special book on discipline
for African American parents?

1. To dispel the violent myths about African American parenting
2. To show how racism negatively affects Black parenting
3. To integrate Black cultural styles and strengths to improve Black parenting
4. To account for parenting differences between Blacks and Whites
5. To improve the psychological future of Black youth

Dispelling the Myths

Why do we need a special book on discipline for African American parents? Well, unfortunately, we have to first dispel the myths about African American parenting styles and child behaviors for all Americans. If we believe the media hype, most African Americans not only physically beat their children, but their children in fact deserve it; and this leads to their becoming violent adults. According to many researchers and the American Academy of Pediatrics (1998), more than 90 percent of all parents admit to using corporal punishment. Most parents report "having used spanking as a means of discipline at some time" (American Academy of Pediatrics, 1998, p. 101). Another study, by Elaine Pinderhughes and others (2000), has found that lower-income persons are more likely to use corporal punishment, which in large measure has to do with being overwhelmed by the stressors of life. Alternative strategies and emotional resources are less likely to be available if you are struggling to make ends meet. These two findings tell us that context matters in the way we apply corporal punishment with our children and that a "quick rush to judgments" will only hinder our understanding of this issue.

We will challenge other misconceptions as part of the larger racism in America that relies on seeing Blacks as animalistic, problematic, and desperately in need of extreme forms of control. These stereotypes are similar to the Black stereotypes in other areas, like women on welfare, men as pimps and pushers, and children and adolescents as violent criminals in the making. Unless we actively challenge these baseless stereotypes, we will be encouraging their acceptance. Black parents differ in the ways they discipline their children. We will present the diversity of struggles and triumphs of Black parenting so that we can undermine the ease with which it is demonized. But still, why do we need a book for and about Black parents and their discipline?

Showing the Effects of Racism

We need this book to identify how a legacy of racism trauma affects African American parenting. To be sure, many African American youth grow up with experiences of spanking and "getting the switch." When African Americans use this type of physical discipline, we often don't realize how we're in sync with a long-held American belief that Black children are not worthy of respect and need to be controlled simply because they are Black and supposedly animalistic. This belief is directly related to historical beliefs that supported African enslavement around the world but particularly in America.

This book will provide self-help tests and easy-to-answer questions that encourage African American parents to recognize racism and discrimination, both blatant and subtle. It would be a mistake to believe that all African Americans understand the hidden ways that the media and the world are racist and discriminatory. Many of us are so traumatized that we simply want to ignore and deny the presence of racism or hope it goes away like a bad smell. Trauma includes the emotions and behaviors that anyone expresses when the pain from a previously unexpected and unfair violation is not healed.

Unfortunately, racism is so psychologically damaging that it can result in our swallowing and believing the stereotypes of Black youth and parenting. This process of "blaming the victim" is an expected psychological reaction to trauma when you are oppressed psychologically over long periods of time with little or no power to combat the oppression. That is why we have to critique these myths.

When Martin Luther King Jr. and Malcolm X were shot, millions mourned the death of two great men, but the most devastating aspect of these killings was not the physical death. It was the psychological assault on the hopefulness of an oppressed people. It was as if hope died on those days. As much as King was preaching, "I have a dream," the trauma was saying, "You don't have the right to dream." The dream for a better life had died, or so we thought. We feared that we would be wandering in the wilderness. Parents must understand this trauma and its impact on themselves and their children, then be prepared for it when—not if—it comes.

Racism through the myths about Black folk is present in all forms of media images from cartoons to movies. We are hard-pressed to find positive images of African Americans on television or the big screen. Why is it that young children will rarely find positive images among cartoons, where White characters are clearly identified as White and African American characters are confusing or alien? Or how is it that the character is clearly identified as African American by language and voice but not by what is seen on the television screen? Or why is it that the African American characters are not the brains of the operation or the hero or heroine who makes the key decisions that solve the problem of the day?

These and other dilemmas are known by a majority of African Americans but rarely are integrated into a cohesive set of parenting strategies. Even when we know that blatant and subtle forms of racism exist, African American parents are often paralyzed when it comes to parenting our children so that they are emotionally protected and able to resist or challenge those images. Far too often our parenting of African American youth is a compilation of fears of what American racism will do to our children, our own anger and hostility at being mistreated so consistently, and our helplessness in the face of this racism. Nevertheless we believe that no form of discipline, whether physical or verbal, that flows from fear, hostility, and helplessness can be positive for our children.

Integrating Black Cultural Style into Parenting

We have to explain the uniqueness of Black cultural style and how it can be integrated into our parenting to improve the parenting of Black youth. We need a book that explains how our language, behavior, and emotional processing are different from those of the majority of American culture of Western European Whites that often represents a skewed and distorted standard against which all other styles are judged.

For example, when a Black parent uses his or her voice in a gruff manner—"Boy, I bet you betta get your butt . . ."—this may be identified by some as abusive without considering how we express ourselves. Being able to pick up on the vibes of others is a talent that many African Americans are trained to learn. So often, understanding how we use our voice, body language, and rhythm and tone of mannerisms is very important to understanding our culture. Unfortunately, these nuances of culture are, at best, unnoticed or, at worst, diagnosed as deviant by White America.

Misinterpreting Black behavior is perhaps the most serious of the many reasons African American parents reject the advice of others, including helping professionals and their books. So why should parents be interested in how to integrate Black cultural style into their parenting? Because Black cultural style is not only different—it is powerful. The irony is that America's business establishments, like McDonald's, Burger King, and Sprite, have acknowledged and exploited the power of Black cultural style by using it in their marketing campaigns for fast food and soft drinks. What if that same power could be harnessed in the development of children so they could appreciate their uniqueness without fearing that they had to hide it from others? Venus and Serena Williams are examples of Black talents who, when on the center stage, appear to appreciate themselves and their cultural uniqueness, unashamed of what the world thinks of them. When they win, they celebrate in age-appropriate, culturally relevant ways. This is possible, in our view, because they have been loved as children of African descent in addition to being loved as children.

Again, to assume that African Americans appreciate their culture and know how to integrate their cultural styles into the parenting process is a big mistake. This diversity and power of cultural style is often minimized by most African Americans except when the stakes of oppression are very high. Our appreciation of cultural style power often only comes out when we are under blatant racial attack. We rarely consider it in day-to-day interactions and behaviors with our children or anyone else. It's like the air that no one questions or the water that fish assume exists without interruption. In this book our goal is to show how parents can use this cultural style to give their children more confidence in themselves through discipline.

The way we will encourage the appreciation of Black culture and style is to provide a framework for parents so they can integrate their culture with their parenting as a resource, not a crutch or a thorn. That framework is based on a very holistic but culturally relevant African religious philosophy. That philosophy suggests that the highest form of knowledge is self-knowledge. If you don't know or appreciate yourself, then you are not likely to appreciate anything or anyone else. *Self* for us includes not just individuals but a cultural community. Self is extended beyond the individual.

Accounting for Parenting Differences Between Blacks and Whites

You will not believe what I saw in the grocery store the other day. This cute little White boy—must have been no more than five years old—was telling his mom he wanted some Rugrats fruit roll-ups or snacks, and his mother had already put two boxes in the shopping cart. Well, he wanted four. And when he didn't get four, he started to yell and scream and call her names like "stupid" and "dumb" and say stuff like "I hate you." Over some fruit snack. I tell you, if my child said that, he would have to pick his lips up off the floor before he could say the word Rugrats—embarrassing me like that. I wish he would. . . . Nooo. That mother got so frustrated, trying to tell him to "talk softly," all nice and sweet-like, and that boy just kept on yelling. Don't you know she picked up two more boxes of Rugrats fruit snacks and put them into the cart just to shut him up? Noooooo. Not my child.

Sarah, age thirty-four, Trenton, New Jersey

⤳

Many Black parents view the parenting of their children in different ways than Whites do. These differences do not exist across the board; not all Black parents raise their children the same way. However, many African American parents and children often comment on the different behavioral styles they see among European American parents. African Americans are often amazed at the amount of disrespect and permissiveness they perceive among White children. We believe that all families struggle with the same challenges of raising children, but they go about them in culturally different ways based on different cultural values.

Language style is one way African American parents differ from other parents in child rearing. To many professionals many Black families can appear to be harsh in their styles of speaking.

Parents from different cultural groups may follow strategies similar to those mentioned in this book. In fact, many White parents have commented that they were raised in environments where the cultural values were similar to those in Black communities. The difference we make here is that racism and racist perceptions could lead to more negative societal control toward an undisciplined child of color, especially in a society that daily misinterprets and punishes the cultural behaviors of Black folk.

Improving Our Children's Psychological Future

A key and final reason we need a book on discipline for African American families and youth is to improve the psychological conditions of Black youth. The larger experiences of African American children are not encouraging. They generally reflect a loss of caring and loving. African American children are showing up in national health statistics that not only reflect society's racism but also point to the fact that children are left alone to battle this world by themselves, without parental involvement.

Many Black youth are situated to manage their life experiences in isolation, and we believe parents can do more. We believe that both poor and affluent African American parents are under more economic pressure than ever before. Some are trying to make ends meet, and others are trying to make sure their finances never end. Both groups are stressed to the max, with time being as precious as money. We believe this pressure and the trauma of racism compromise the time and energy available for managing the complexities of raising Black children.

In our view African Americans can't afford to just *do* parenting; we have to *think* and *feel* about it too. We believe that discipline without self-knowledge is self-destructive. In fact, discipline without a lot of key ingredients is self-destructive. Can you fill in the blank in the following list? We have our suggestions. Do you have any?

Discipline without _____ *is self-destructive.*

---

1. Knowledge of my individual and collective selves

2. A committed relationship

3. Accountability

4. Love

5. Protection

6. A village

HOW THIS BOOK IS PUT TOGETHER

Effective Black parenting involves the integration of cultural coping and cultural pride. It involves viewing discipline as an extension of loving Black youth, not as something you do when the world has mistreated you. The success of our future depends on it. We will provide information on how to discipline children from infancy through high school in culturally relevant and appreciating ways. We will help parents reflect on their own childhood as well as on how they were disciplined as children and how that impacts their parenting now.

The first chapter will focus on whether parents know themselves and on how they care for themselves. Through mini self-tests and fill-in-the-blank responses, parents will be able to judge how much they know about their needs, their history, their stories. The remaining chapters move from preschool through the teenage years and provide advice on how to discipline youth in these very different developmental periods. How do you stick to, watch over, and get with a two-year-old as opposed to a ten-year-old? What should you expect from a two-year-old, and how can a parent integrate cultural coping, pride, and self-knowledge into one's discipline so that the child will make sense of his or her world?

Because parenting is a lifelong acquaintance with helplessness, disciplining children must take multiple routes. Some of us scold, some of us do time-outs, some of us spank, and some of us have long-winded never ending conversations. Some of us never scold, spank, or give time-outs. We are not going to tell you that any of these work best, but we are going to give you guidelines you can use in making choices. We are going to tell you what we think works best and when, depending on the age and developmental needs of the child.

The hardest job for any parent is raising their children to become caring adults, but for African American parents the obstacles are often related not to their abilities but to what others think of them. Integrating the material and the spiritual realities of the world is so important for our little ones. This book will help parents understand these issues and feel less helpless about parenting and disciplining an African American child. As we have already mentioned, the biblical phrase "Spare the rod and spoil the child" is an old saying in the Black community. But we suggest its basic biblical reference is rooted in parents knowing themselves, knowing their child, knowing their culture and community, and knowing their Creator. To see this phrase as a justification for spanking is not only missing the mark; it's like shooting arrows with your teeth. You can try it, but you never really know if your aim is good. Proverbs 29:15 says, "The rod of correction imparts wisdom, but a child left to himself disgraces his mother." To spare the rod does not mean withholding spanking but, rather, denying our children the wisdom of affection, protection, and correction they need to understand the full meaning of discipline and who they are.

"Spare not the rod" means

---

1. Sparing not the affection
2. Sparing not the protection
3. Sparing not the accountability

But one point is essential to remember: African American parents cannot let someone else tell their children who they are. And as parents, we cannot tell them who they are until we know who we are as individuals and as a people. African American parents cannot afford to be ignorant of our cultural and individual histories if we want to create a new future for our children. The phrase "It's a tough job, but somebody has to do it" is only half true. That "somebody" can only be us.

So let's take a look at "us" as the first step in learning effective discipline. Do you know who *you* are—as a person, not a parent? Your first name is not Mommy or Daddy. You had or have aspirations and goals that didn't include children. What were they? What are they?

You had a childhood, and you received discipline. You were a child once, remember? And you have a story to tell. Our first step in learning effective discipline begins with ourselves and the stories we could tell (but too often don't). If a "lion's story will never be known as long as the hunter is the one to tell it," dear parent, what is your story? You can begin to tell us in Chapter One.

For Parents Only

Stickin' To, Watchin' Over, and Gettin' With Thyself

The tyrant is only the slave turned inside out.

Think about myself? I don't have time to think about myself. If I take care of my child, I'm takin' care of myself. If I don't take care of them first, I won't feel good anyway. If I had to do it all over again, maybe I would have followed my dreams and had my kids later, but I made my choice a long time ago. Being a parent means wrapping up your dreams and packing them away. I made my bed, and now I have to lie in it. I love my kids, and they'll always come first.

❧

When we speak to a group of parents, we ask them if they would want their children to stay up late, get hardly any sleep, act "evil" toward classmates, look tired and worn down at school or church, and ignore their body's warning signals until they get sick. The answer is always "No way!" Yet when we ask them to examine their own lives, they admit that this describes their own lifestyles.

Children learn how to care for themselves by watching their parents. It's scary to think that children watch and imitate what we do and how we live. They not only watch what we do, but they watch how we do it with others. So you can imagine how important the relationships we choose are. Thus another key aspect of parenting is considering the adult relationships we are involved with. How we treat ourselves and allow others to treat us are two sides to the same coin in the eyes of our children.

Ever see your child mimic your gestures, language, or hand movements? Even when they don't seem to be paying attention, they watch us like hawks and will take what they see to heart. In this chapter we want to give parents strategies for knowing when and how to be ready for the endless ways Black youth will need them. How do children learn to love themselves? How do they learn to be patient, kind, and caring? Yes, you know the answer. Most of what they learn is from us. Just think of your own childhood and who people say you act like the most. Is it true that "you're just like your parents"? These and other questions make parenting one of the hardest jobs to do—because the questions never stop coming. If we want to know who our children are, then we have to know ourselves first.

In African religious philosophy, *self-knowledge* is the greatest knowledge one can achieve. We believe that African American parents have to manage many selves—individual selves (me, myself, and I) and cultural selves (me, you, and us). This self-knowledge involves how much you know and appreciate the past, present, and future experiences of your life and culture and the lives and culture of your people. For African American parents, becoming very well acquainted with our personal and cultural selves is winning half the battle. So although we talk about the importance of affection, correction, and protection for children, the most important lesson is that parents must apply these principles to themselves *first*. If this happens, then they should expect to see the maximum benefit from these ingredients in their children. So how do parents stick to, watch over, and get with themselves?

How do you stick to, watch over, and get with yourself?

1. Know your individual self.

2. Know your cultural self.

KNOWING YOUR INDIVIDUAL SELF

❧

*If you know what hurts yourself, you know what
hurts others.*

❧

A person who does not know and appreciate himself or herself is
less likely to treat others with care and concern and more likely to
act out or hurt other people—especially children. A parent without adequate self-knowledge is like a gardener without garden tools.
They may have the ability, but they have to work twice as hard to
get half as much results.

Parents who lack personal self-knowledge may

1. Act out past childhood pains through their parenting
2. Expect their children to behave like adults
3. Fail to separate personal needs from their children's
   needs
4. React to children with a short fuse and an evil eye
5. See the world in "either-or" instead of "both-and"
   terms

What do we expect to see in parents who lack personal self-
knowledge? Well, it doesn't take a rocket scientist or a psychologist
to figure this out. Over time, without this self-awareness, parents are
likely to do one or more of a number of things. One outcome of self-
ignorance is to live out one's childhood through his or her child's life
experiences. The buying of toys (say, around Christmas) or the pur-
chasing of clothes can become the arena where one seeks to rehabil-
itate one's broken childhood. The parent's inner child is screaming,
"I wish I could have had these things when I was a child!"

Another result of self-ignorance is that parents may begin to confide in their children as adults or expect them to understand their adult life experiences. When children are unable to meet the emotional demands of parents who are lacking in self-knowledge (and all children are unable to meet these demands), parents feel even more isolated. When this occurs, parents may withdraw their affection to save whatever they have for themselves. In some female-headed households sons can play different roles, including child, buddy, protector, and therapist. These roles can be unhealthy when they become overwhelming for the child or when the child's own childhood needs are not being met (for example, if the child is not making same-age friends or is not learning how to handle conflicts with peers).

How can these kinds of problems be avoided? How can we become better parents by knowing our own strengths and weaknesses? There are several steps in getting to know your individual self.

How to Know Your Individual Self

1. Know the warning signs of excess personal baggage.
2. Lighten your excess personal baggage and ask for help.
3. Strengthen and lengthen the end of your emotional rope.
4. Become a "both-and" parent.

Know the Warning Signs of Excess Personal Baggage

Frequently Asked Questions

"Will somebody tell me because I may not be Bill Cosby, but I'm doing the best I can!"

- What do I do when I get overwhelmed?

- If I can't control my temper, what should I say to my child after I calm down?

- What has helped me to calm my anger in the past?

- What can I say to the people around me after I am angry?

- How come I am the one that gets all the flak?

Have you ever seen someone who has taken a vacation with too much luggage? You may see them in the airport or bus station and notice that they have little awareness of the people around them. Why? Because they are overwhelmed with their belongings. They are either overly apologetic or oblivious to others because their bags are so weighty. When they move with all of their luggage, you can see that look of anxiety and fatigue on their faces. The fatigue comes from having to deal with their decision to carry so much. Anxiety comes from the possibility that they might have made a bad decision, or worse—some of their personal belongings may be lost.

Personal baggage is very similar. It is heavy because it is connected to a past that is often hard to get over. It still weighs you down. And it is complex. You may not understand why you sometimes become so angry with your child, but in fact he may remind you of someone you had difficulty with in the past or someone you are having trouble with now. Maybe the feeling of helplessness is so hard to handle because it reminds you of past abuses, humiliations, or difficult situations. Who knows? *You know.* But it takes time to admit it to yourself. It may take a while to uncover past pain, but your children will feel safer if you try. If you identify your personal baggage and prevent it from undermining your parenting, you will be giving your children a wonderful gift.

Child in the "Hood"

Most parents think that once they are adults, they leave their childhood behind, but nothing could be further from the truth. You can take the inner child from the "hood," but you can never take the childhood out of your heart. This fact, although quite easy to understand, is one of the most misunderstood and forgotten facts known to parenting and adulthood. For some reason adults selectively forget what their childhood was like, especially when they have kids. And why not? Although many of the memories are priceless, some are, frankly, worth forgetting.

Childhood is a time when you are outsized, outnumbered, outpowered, and outthought by almost everybody, including other children, so where's the fun in that? Psychologically, this is at least a stressful experience; children with parents who don't understand this stress or forget about it are less likely to get help to deal with the stress. Black children whose parents are also unaware of the racial stressors of childhood may feel more pressure to survive childhood.

One of the ways children survive childhood is to play a role that satisfies the family's overall needs. For some families children play the mediator or psychologist. Some children play the rebel. Some play the weak, innocent one or the "do-gooder." Whichever role we play, the role is often meant to distract us from the larger tensions in the family, the neighborhood, or the society at large. When these tensions go unresolved, children carry them into their adulthood. The pains of childhood are often the emotional ingredients of bad parenting.

So trauma experiences could have occurred when you were expected to be a "real man" before you were ten by showing you could take a spanking without crying, when one of your parents called you out in front of all of your friends, or when you got a spanking from the playground all the way home. These experiences may all be part of that unresolved pain. It does not affect some parents. But for others the memory sits and hovers like a computer virus waiting to mess up their parenting. So if you remember that you were treated unfairly as a child, you can deal with it by turning those experiences into a "plus" or a "minus." But whether those experiences are perceived as a plus or a minus, you might fail to resolve their importance to you. Some parents will take a plus and include it in their parenting as a "necessary evil" or take a minus and never apply strategies like it, considering it unnecessary under any circumstances. This rigid style of parenting reflects parents who did not survive childhood well, and that fact comes out in their parenting.

One example is parents who fail to discipline because they feel being harsh can hurt their children and who thus become so permissive that their children fail to feel safe and to understand appropriate boundaries. The minus of being humiliated as a child has been carried into parenting and leads to excessive permissiveness and the abdication of discipline. An example of a plus is parents who feel their beatings helped them and who, without questioning their childhood experience, automatically resort to the use of physical punishment, not fully knowing why or caring what effect the strategy has on their children. The belief is "My daddy spanked me, and I turned out all right. It's a good thing because my daddy was a good man, and that's all I need to know."

How do you know if something is unresolved from your childhood? Well, it often depends on how rigid you are about your parenting. If you think something has to be done the same way all the time and are unable to give up on your view or at least talk about an alternative, you may just be carrying excess personal baggage. If you find that you start telling childhood stories that have no particular focus or meaning, you may be trying to recover your childhood. If you get furious about little matters for no reason or you use your children as minitherapists, you just might be reliving your childhood through your parenting.

Warning Signs of Excess Personal Baggage

1. You have flashbacks of childhood experiences while thinking freely or driving.

2. You instantly get furious at something your child does, and you have no idea why.

3. You start referring to stories of your own childhood so often that your children say, "Oh, Lord, here we go again."

4. Your childhood stories don't have a focus or a lesson attached to them.

5. You find that you are willing to fight to the death over a small issue (like which way the toilet paper should roll).

6. You talk to your child as if he or she were your personal therapist.

7. You defend your parents' discipline strategies way too much.

Defending Our Parents' Form of Discipline

I can remember as a child saying to myself that when I grow up I'll never do this or that to my children. I promised myself I would not—no, could not—treat my children the way my parents treated me. Now I sometimes hear myself saying the same words to my children that my mother used to say to me!

Why do most people defend spanking by their parents when the topic comes up? Well, there are several reasons, but the key reason is that we love our parents. The reasons why people are reluctant to critique the spanking behavior of their parents often come from this one simple fact. Another reason is that spanking does not happen outside of a relationship or relationship context. If a stranger physically reprimands a child for negative behavior, it's not called "spanking," it's called "assault and battery." No, spanking mostly happens within a history of parental caring and frustration, and children (even adult children) will defend this relationship, whether it worked for them or not. To critique the spanking is to critique the loving parent, and few of us want to do that.

Many of us have cultural rules that say, "A child should never question the authority of a parent. Never!" And this includes never challenging a parent's motivations for discipline in conversation, in writing, or even in one's own heart, mind, and soul. Ironically, children are going to defend their parents even in the most abusive of situations. Studies have shown that physically and sexually abused children protect the image of their parents when they are young; not to protect the abusive parent is to somehow fail to protect oneself.

This is where the statement "I got spanked, and I turned out fine" comes in. Often we judge our parents as "good parents" using gross rather than fine examples of proof. We defend our parents based on statements like "They loved me" or "I am still alive." We look at the larger outcomes and less at the finer emotional life consequences and find it hard to be too critical.

Ten Things Adults Say to Defend Their Own Parents' Discipline

1. "They loved me."
2. "I'm still alive, ain't I?"
3. "I got spanked, and I turned out fine."
4. "I got over it."
5. "They were doing the best they could."
6. "They had a lot of things on their mind."
7. "They were trying to teach me a lesson."
8. "I was a bad kid. They had to spank me."
9. "If I was them, I would do the same thing."
10. "I'd rather them discipline me than society."

Lighten Your Excess Personal Baggage and Ask for Help

The first thing to admit to yourself is "I am overwhelmed." It is absolutely normal for all parents to feel helpless and overwhelmed, so give yourself the space to say it. You know what alcohol counselors say to folks who have drinking problems? They say the first step is admitting that you have a problem. Well, parents may not think they have a problem, but they do have feelings of being overwhelmed. Not admitting it can turn into a big problem. Remember what we said: *parenting is a lifelong acquaintance with helplessness.* So it happens to all of us, over and over again. If you admit your helplessness, then you can begin to deal with it by asking the question, "How do I ask for help?" Questions that parents often ask themselves about the past include the following:

Frequently Asked Questions

- What do I remember about how my parents raised me?

- What still angers me about what my parents did?

- Do I let my anger about my parents' behaviors influence how I raise my children?

- What behaviors in my parenting are the same as my parents'?

- What do I do about spanking my children? I got family that says I do it too much, and some say I'm too easy. Who's right?

- I got spanked, and I turned out all right. Why do I feel so bad after I do it, though?

- Is there a time when spanking is okay?

Self-knowledge is primarily possible through identifying past pains and traumas. With this type of knowledge, it seems parents will have an edge when the same problems arise in their children. Not to be aware of these psychological pains can leave parents unable to help children manage their emotional stressors. So we recommend that, in order to lighten your load, you identify past trauma.

Well, the first step in knowing your individual self is identifying the excess personal baggage that you carry with you every day. After realizing that your personal baggage is too heavy, the next step is to face your past and ask for help.

Strengthen and Lengthen the End of Your Emotional Rope

∞

At the gate of patience there is no overcrowding.

∞

It's easy to go off on one of my kids when I'm stressed out. It takes effort to count to ten or go to my room and cool out for a while. It also takes time to restrain oneself not to have that knee-jerk reaction where you just turn around and before you know it, you're yelling at the top of your lungs. The reality is there never seems to be any space to breathe. There is always something else that has to be done first. And when it's all said and done, I'm too tired to do anything except fall into bed and wake up stressed again the next morning.

∞

Do you know when you have reached your frustration point— when your child has trampled on your last nerve? You probably know: when you are about to call your child so many names and the only thing that comes out is "@#^!*>$." We think there ought to be a word like this ("@#^!*>$") in the dictionary just for parents who get frustrated with their children. And when we reach the end of our rope, it's usually *because* we love our kids and *because* we are so involved in their lives.

Being frustrated is no crime. We all get there. Been there, done that. In fact, there are studies that show that parents spend a lot of their time in anger because of the challenges of parenting. Being angry is not the problem! Letting the anger fester and get sore is the problem. The problem lies in not addressing one's frustration by getting or asking for help. Children are often a less powerful group (or so we think) whom we can easily use to deal with our sense of helplessness. When we don't get help for our problems, the real problem comes when we take out our anger on our children.

What does a parent at the end of her rope do? Walk away. Count to ten. Call a friend. Play a game. Do whatever it takes to allow yourself time to think. Join activities and organizations that teach you more about yourself or that are fun and relaxing or both. Knowing yourself and what calms you is one of the greatest gifts you can give your child. Just like knowing when you have excess personal baggage, it is important that you know when you are at the end of your rope.

Five Signs That You Have Reached the End of Your Parental Rope

1. You are so frustrated that you can't immediately remember your child's name or you call her the name of every other child you have or know before you finally get to hers.

2. The only thing you can think about is how badly your child has embarrassed you.

3. You believe your child has plotted your public frustration for days, maybe months, and has patiently waited until now to enact the plan.

4. You think that your young child is laughing at your helplessness instead of the funny wrinkles and looks of frustration on your face.

5. You have spoken the Lord's name at least ten times in the last five seconds.

Raising Black children is burdensome enough without having to carry a ton of past pain and sorrow. *Ask for help!* The key to resolving this lifestyle of defensiveness is to face the fact that your parents didn't always get it right. Failure to face this is akin to missing the forest for the trees. Sometimes their strategies worked, and sometimes they didn't. Facing this reality allows you to loosen up as a parent and see the forest as well as the trees. We have heard it said that you can't bury something that isn't dead yet. But if you can face certain painful realities from childhood, it is possible to move them from the "present" issues category to the "past" issues category. Feelings of being abused do not disappear because your parents were good people. Feelings of humiliation do not go away just because someone close to you says, "Get over it." Bury it dead, not alive. The only way to do that is to look at the pain directly.

You can bury it by talking it out to close friends who care and will allow you to express the pain without accusation. You can bury unresolved pain by talking to a therapist who, unlike your children, actually has expertise in this area. Finally, you can bury past pain by asking for help from key people, like your pastor, your Creator, or your church. Forgiveness is possible but not without facing the trauma head-on.

Become a "Both-And" Parent

I'm just doing the best I can, and sometimes that don't feel good enough. It's hard being a good parent and a bad parent all at the same time. Sometimes I am in charge, and some days I need help. Just the other day, my child asked me if I was all right. Now, you know that don't make sense. Here it is, I am the parent, and this child is taking care of me. She seems so wise sometimes. Maybe I can learn from her too. Like that Bible saying—"And a little child shall lead them."

⁓

Unfortunately, one of the hardest lessons to learn about knowing yourself is appreciating both your talents *and* your flaws. So a key skill in parenting Black youth is knowing the difference between "either-or" and "both-and" parenting. That is, we believe that life is made up of positive and negative experiences and that learning from both is necessary for survival and growth. We also believe that our gifts can be liabilities and our liabilities can be gifts. A "both-and" worldview means that all of us are both smart at some things and incompetent at others, that we are both assertive and shy, and that we may be very assertive and directive in one situation but unable to follow or be led in other situations. One example of this is when parents are strong and assertive with their children or with coworkers. But coworkers might be surprised to see these same individuals turn into scared little puppies when they are with their own parents.

Seeing life in both-and terms is different from seeing life as a set of "either-or" experiences where only good or bad things happen to us. African Americans have often been stereotyped into either good or bad categories by society, and we believe this process is at the heart of many forms of racism—to promote one culture as better than another. We must be especially aware that these self-destructive dynamics primarily come from separating our negative and positive aspects. Skin color politics is a great example where African Americans continue to separate based on stereotype.

∽

Being angry is not the problem!
The problem comes from not dealing
with your frustration.

∽

Too often, American society is absolutely wrong when it interprets the potential and motivations of African Americans simply by watching actors on television or seeing real people in one dramatic or unusual instance. This knowledge suggests that individuals are either "good" or "bad." We think that this either-or thinking tends to minimize very important, complex aspects of reality. We also believe that it places parents in a position of making judgments about others and themselves that are either-or.

For instance, we tend to think of babies and parents as good or bad, depending on how much public pain or humiliation they cause us. Rarely do we seek to blend the opposites together in one person and see that every individual embodies the "good" and the "bad." In reality we are skillful at some activities and fairly dull at others. Or we are calm about some events and anxious about others. This is both-and. This principle is another key value in African religious and psychological philosophy and assumes that humans are best understood as a combination of different and complex characteristics.

Examples of Either-Or Beliefs

1. Believing that there are only two kinds of parents: "good" and "bad"

2. Believing that once you make a mistake, there are no second chances

3. Believing as a parent that one is too old to learn about life from a child

4. Believing that a parent has to be either a friend or a disciplinarian

5. Believing that discipline only involves tough love

Either-or thinking may lock parents into using ineffective strategies when disciplining their child. For instance, a child may appear to be both disrespectful and crying out for help. A parent who only reads the outside demeanor may not pick up on the nonverbal signals and may provide ineffective discipline. When parents see themselves as both "good" and "bad" parents, many doors for improvement are open. By seeing oneself as effective in some but not in other areas of discipline, it is easier for a parent to ask for help in weaker areas.

African American parents are often torn between balancing career aspirations and family survival, between basic needs like feeding their families and higher-order needs like self-growth. But if you tend to view parenting experiences as either-or, or win-lose, it can be a problem. Once you start to view life this way, you're likely to feel depressed about how much you lose and insecure that your wins are only temporary. This either-or mentality tends to breed needless insecurity. Either-or parenting is a weak attempt to make the complex simple. We know our children well, and yet we are often shocked at what they show us. Sometimes we feel that we are only one step ahead of our child, if that. When you think about it, there is this amazing irony: we are raising our children in very intimate ways so that they can one day leave us! We make all of this investment so that they can walk away from us.

Sometimes we can't always see the benefits from what we give to our children. In fact, we often give when getting back is nowhere to be found. But parenting is not a give-and-take experience. It's mostly give-give-give-and-maybe-take. This can be confusing to weary parents who need and expect to see the benefits of their hard work immediately. But we believe it pays off in the end. No, our efforts are not in vain. By spending the energy and time, we are building hope for tomorrow. The lessons we teach our children may seem like they go in one ear and out the other, but children are always listening and watching. That's why if we don't take care of ourselves, they learn how to not take care of themselves. If we let others abuse us, they learn how to let others abuse them. Our commitment to love and discipline our children will also teach us lessons about living too.

Examples of Both-And Beliefs

1. Feeling both confident and helpless about parenting

2. Knowing life lessons can come from children as well as parents

3. Believing that parenting involves being a friend *and* a disciplinarian

4. Believing that parenting involves tough *and* soft love
5. Applying affection and protection with correction

Love is a both-and experience too. It's like while you will always love your children, *there are times when you just do not like them!* Sometimes we are managing their behavior wonderfully, and other days we are totally confused about what will work best. This confusion can be tiring and overwhelming. If it continues, feeling overwhelmed can lead us to become either-or parents.

When we simply do what comes easiest and what will reduce our stress the quickest, we give away our power. Because life tends not to be so black and white, we want to identify these both-and realities so parents can sustain the power they will need to manage their children effectively. We must strive to include fewer either-or strategies in our parenting if we want our children to manage themselves in the world as it is: complex, not simple.

Another both-and example is that children who live in our neighborhoods may not be blood relatives of ours but can still benefit from our supervision. As adults in the African American community, *we are still family* to the children in our communities. The late Robin Harris, an African American comedian, used to talk about the children of a woman whom he called "Bay-Bay." He called them "Bay-Bay's kids." These kids were notorious for destruction, mayhem, and having knowledge well beyond their years. No one liked them, and no one wanted to baby-sit them because they were so rowdy. Well, in a both-and world, even Bay-Bay's kids are our kids! All of these "bad" kids are *our* kids—especially if we see family as more than blood relations and if we realize that we have a larger responsibility to sustain community survival.

These are not new values to African Americans, just forgotten ones. They can still become the ingredients of a discipline strategy that serves children, families, and neighborhoods. Raising children is not just what parents do but what the "village" does. And kids don't become Bay-Bay's kids overnight. Both-and thinking can help us know our children and ourselves.

KNOWING YOUR CULTURAL SELF

⁓

Through others I am somebody. I am because we are.

⁓

Many African American parents want their children to know about their cultural roots but, frankly, don't know where to begin. It sometimes feels like you are begging your children to be a certain kind of Black person. Or sometimes it feels like as soon as you start talking about cultural pride issues, all discussions lead back to Martin Luther King Jr. because we don't know as much about our cultural history as possible. You may find it difficult to talk to your child about Africa when you're living in Philadelphia. You may find yourself becoming bitter when you talk to your child about race because it raises up your own past experiences of unresolved racial pain.

Unresolved racial pain has the same effect on one's parenting as the emotional pain of one's childhood. Before we can expect African American parents to teach children about their racial and cultural heritage, parents must explore their own racial histories and experiences first.

How to Know Your Collective, Cultural Self

1. Face your cultural fears (of being Black).
2. Give your children cultural pride reinforcement.
3. Raise a village.

Face Your Cultural Fears

What does it mean to know our cultural selves? It means knowing and being aware of the reality of our cultural existence in America. It means facing our tragedies as well as our triumphs, the pains as well as the promises. It means asking ourselves a series of questions to manage the burden of parenting Black children. Parents of African American children must ask themselves the following key questions:

Questions African American Parents Can Use to Know Their Cultural Selves

1. What do I fear will happen to my child because he or she is Black?

2. What do I do when I am afraid, angry, and helpless to protect my child from harm or danger? From racial harm or danger?

3. How do these feelings and actions of fear, anger, and helplessness seep into my discipline strategies?

4. Am I hard on my children because I want to prepare them for how the world will be hard on them?

5. Am I soft on my children because I don't want them to get discouraged from the racial hostility the world will dump on them?

If you answered yes to one or both of questions 4 and 5, then you are most likely parenting from a victim's position. You should review and explain your answers to questions 1 through 3 more carefully with a trusted family member or friend. Or at least write them down and reflect on them as you read the rest of this book. This reflection on your feelings and actions, communication of your feelings to trusted ones, and letting go of your fears are essential so that you can limit how much they sneak out and communicate to your children that you are afraid of them, angry at them, and helpless to protect them.

In a world of hateful myths about Black people, healthy parenting exists when we reframe our fears, hostility, and helplessness into proactive, culturally relevant, pride-reinforcing strategies. There are several key strategies to help parents get over the paralysis that comes when they don't know how to talk to their children, when they are fearful of racial hostility, when discipline is required, and when protection, affection, and correction have to be applied at the same time.

Parents who lack racial self-knowledge may

1. Fail to identify racial unfairness and discrimination when they occur

2. Deny and mismanage their emotional trauma reactions to racism

3. Fail to prepare their children to manage the emotional trauma of racism

4. Adopt and integrate negative societal racist attitudes in their parenting

5. Fail to encourage children's positive racial self-esteem

In contrast, personally and racially aware parents can identify the complexity of these developmental and racial politics and judge more accurately. Why? Because their eyes are wide open instead of "wide shut." When you know your personal strengths and weaknesses, you are better able to use alternative strategies when you get overwhelmed. You are able to recognize the behaviors and emotions that signal when stress is getting the best of you. Aware parents will panic less when they feel helpless and will realize that helplessness is not a disease but a normal reaction to the enormous task of raising children.

Parents who do not know or appreciate their culture can make hasty and inaccurate decisions for their children in a climate of racial hostility. A racially unaware parent misinterprets the developmental and racial politics that children go through.

Racially aware parents will be able to identify when unfairness is subtle and blatant and respond with multiple well-thought-out strategies. They will also be able to teach their children how to manage these inevitable conflicts, using courage, self-protection, and self-respect. "The tyrant is only the slave turned inside out" is meant to represent the way many racially unaware African American parents may inadvertently adopt the negative racist percetions concerning African Americans in their child discipline strategies. The use of physical discipline without knowing the potential emotional damage it may have on children is related to an enslaved mentality. According to this mentality, African Americans are not worthy of the best things in life (including the best emotional and mental health). This mind-set can unwittingly encourage self-dehumanization.

Teach yourself by going to local African American bookstores and businesses that promote cultural heritage in advertising and products. Identify these establishments in your neighborhood or surrounding area. Ask other parents about the best places to get the latest cultural information. Where do you shop for art? When you shop for Black art, do you know the background of the artist as well as the story behind the work that you have either bought or plan to buy? Which Black art do you like the most, and why do those themes interest you more than others? You don't have to have money to buy Black art. Buying calendars with Black art can cost less than $5. The panels of each month can then be cut, framed, and hung up for practically nothing. Hang them up! Making these themes available to your child is important, but what is more important is that you know why you want to make these themes available.

Join a professional organization that is pro-Black. Howard Stevenson is a former president of a local chapter of Black psychologists. The benefits of joining and actively participating in such a group, besides the contacts and professional development, include the overwhelming relief that comes with not having to explain or censor or mute one's cultural language, style, or expression. There is a healing that comes from just being your "Black" self, however that is expressed, without the fear that your colleagues will devalue your professional talents.

Give Your Children Cultural Pride Reinforcement

Because African American parents must discipline their children in a racially ambivalent society, applying normal parenting advice may be necessary but is insufficient. That's why we recommend cultural pride reinforcement (CPR). CPR includes parents' teaching children how to feel good about themselves and their cultural heritage. We affectionately call it "CPR" because we believe cultural knowledge is so vital to the psychological and emotional lifeblood of African Americans that its absence is cause for alarm. When someone is physically debilitated, you apply cardiopulmonary resuscitation; when someone is psychologically or culturally and emotionally debilitated, you apply cultural pride reinforcement.

Many African American children are emotionally and psychologically assaulted every day in a world that believes they are incapable of success. Over time this assault can cause harm. Our research has shown that CPR is invaluable to helping Black youth survive racial oppression and stress. Effective discipline for African American families requires an active racial socialization focus of which CPR is the primary component. What is racial socialization? It is a combination of conversations and actions that communicate to our children how to survive with dignity and pride in a racist world.

The role of resistance as a cultural value in African American communities is not restricted to adult behavior but reflects the community's views as well. We pay special attention to the heritage of storytelling about race that goes on directly and indirectly in African American families. Racial storytelling includes the ways Black parents teach their children to endure racial hostility and develop racial pride as they live in a world that despises them. Research demonstrates that this racial storytelling, or "racial socialization" as some call it, is essential to the psychological health of African Americans. In particular, we know that there are two major types of messages that parents use to communicate to their children about culture, race, racism, and race relations: *protective* racial socialization and *proactive* racial socialization.

Protective parenting regarding race and culture involves messages and interactions with children about how to survive life by dealing with racial oppression. These messages include "You have to work twice as hard as the next person to get ahead because you are Black." Proactive cultural messages and interactions communicate to children how to survive life by appreciating and embracing the creative and healing aspects of their cultural heritage without worrying about oppression or what Whites think about Blacks. Too much of the "Watch out for those who will hurt you" message without the "Be proud of who you are and where you come from" message can be challenging to young souls and spirits that need to be creative and dream as well as be wary and vigilant. Unfortunately, research shows that only half of Black families directly discuss racism and how to deal with it.

Protective Racial Messages Parents Say to Their Children

1. "You have to work twice as hard to get ahead because you are Black."

2. "Some people may not like you because of the color of your skin, but don't give up."

3. "Life is not fair, but you can still overcome."

We believe that discipline must be understood within both protective and proactive racial socialization orientations. To discipline from a perspective of protection alone will often leave parents too desperate about "saving children from a hostile world" and lead them to underemphasize their children's need for nurturance. On the other hand, to communicate only proactive racial messages may be helpful for the child to understand his or her potential in the world while appreciating his or her cultural or bicultural heritage but may not prepare the child psychologically for racial oppression, should it occur. We believe that parents need to think about discipline from both protective (resistance-to-oppression focus) and proactive (promotion-of-cultural-empowerment focus) orientations in order for our children to grow healthy, wealthy, and wise.

Marguerite Wright's book (1998) raises a concern about the problem of projecting racial anger and fear on young children. This may be too much for a child to handle at young ages, so knowing the developmental challenges is key when parents are teaching about cultural pride or racial injustice. This explains exactly why parents must process their own personal racial issues in order to focus their teaching on the child's needs, not their own unresolved racial pain. Sometimes young children struggle with skin color issues at the level of color differences, not at the level of racial and social injustice or inequality. They should be allowed to explore those differences free of parental fear that their child is racially illiterate. So we believe that understanding discipline in a cultural context makes it more effective than if it is understood as an isolated event like spanking.

Proactive Racial Messages Parents Say to Their Children

1. "You are wonderfully and beautifully made."
2. "Be proud of your Blackness and your heritage."
3. "You have a heritage that comes from African royalty."

> 4. "You can be whatever you want to be."
> 5. "Your culture gives you a wisdom that no one else has."
> 6. "Trusting in God can overcome all things."

We know that parents discipline with the future in mind and often do so in case they are not alive when their children get older. Giving your children CPR allows them life-saving, self-appreciating, and community-embracing psychological strategies that have survived centuries of oppression.

So what does a racially aware CPR parent do? One strategy is to buy books and magazines that reflect a diversity of the color spectrum of people in the country. Buying magazines that feature African American women and men of various skin tones, from dark to light, as the main characters is important. Read young children stories and folktales about racial conflicts and how the main characters use ingenious, clever ways to outwit a more powerful foe. Ask children question about the television shows they watch and point out the subtle assumptions of Black inferiority inherent in many television shows and sitcoms. Another entertaining way to teach cultural pride is when children begin to show you commercials and sitcom logic doesn't make sense to them based on your criteria of respectful CPR programming. Parents can point out who the heroes and heroines are in cartoons and who they often tend to be and why, or they can remark on how wonderful it is when Black actors are the problem solvers as well as the heroes and heroines.

Buy, play, and teach your children about different forms of music by Black artists, and teach them about how old forms of music are related to newer forms (like how jazz is connected to hip-hop or slave songs are connected to freedom and defiance of racial injustice). Stevie Wonder has a wonderful song called "Black Man," where he writes of different African Americans, Native Americans, Latino Americans, and White Americans who created practical everyday inventions. The authors grew up on Stevie Wonder, who was a master at teaching about life, social injustice, and cultural history in his songs, which were at the same time rhythmically contemporary and cool. You could dance and pop your fingers to Stevie while, without even realizing it, you learned about your culture at the same time.

Take your child to people who know things that you don't know. Expose them to Black wax museums, cultural history museums and exhibits, or Web sites where there are opportunities to both play and learn. The biggest thing you can do is learn and read new information yourself because it will model for your child what he or she can do later on. Also, your teaching will become natural instead of "staged" if you are teaching what comes from your experiences rather than what comes from some book.

Raise a Village

Frequently Asked Questions

- How can I make sure that my parental values and behaviors are carried out by the people who help watch my children?

- What kind of talents do I want my child to be exposed to?

Although many politicians and family advocates have been borrowing the African proverb "It takes a village to raise a child," they are rarely able to move beyond slogans to help parents understand what a village is. The real question behind this proverb is, "What does it take to raise a healthy village?" The key ingredients for raising a healthy village include the different groups of people whom parents can connect with and who will agree to help them in their parenting.

We know what you are thinking: "Today who can you trust?" Parents are rightfully frightened about whom to leave their children with. But the alternative is often more frightening. And often the tough work is checking potential baby-sitters out. The notion that one parent can work, raise children and attend to all of the children's emotional needs, and handle the challenges of catastrophe is still prevalent across America, but any parents under these circumstances will tell you that they would like help.

Consider the following scenario:

Jerry was shoveling snow one day when he heard a child's voice in the distance yelling at other boys to stop hitting him. When Jerry turned around, he saw that two neighborhood boys were throwing snow at another boy with such energy that it seemed like a fight. The boy was crying out loud as if he was in serious pain. Being the Good Samaritan, Jerry yelled out at the two boys to stop. All of a sudden, all three boys cursed at him and began throwing snowballs at Jerry. After quickly running into the house for safety, Jerry wondered whether he should ever help out a neighbor again.

❧

What does Jerry do in a situation like this? Should he give up and never help out again? No, instead we think he needs to go one step further. He needs to call up the parents of these boys and tell their parents. It's quite possible that their parents may be just as negative and closed to anything he has to say. But it is also possible that they might appreciate someone who cared enough to "tell on" the boys so that their behaviors can be corrected immediately.

So how does discipline work if all of the components are put together well?

❧

If you love the children of others, you will love your own even better.

❧

It used to be thought that single parenting was a sin and a crime. Some politicians and researchers still believe this. The fact of the matter is that it is a lot harder to do it on your own. *Nobody* has ever parented their children by themselves and done as well as when there is someone else around to help. Those parents who are forced to do so, must be commended for their sustenance and praised for doing what is the most difficult job on the face of the earth.

What's equally true, however, is that it takes more than two persons to raise a child, so those who want to tout two-parent homes as better than one-parent homes ought to consider that our children are raised by teachers, blood relatives, adult neighbors, ministers, coaches, non–blood relatives, mentors, baby-sitters, and youth leaders. There is no crime in admitting that raising children is a community process.

Okay, now if you admit that "it takes a village," what do you think happens when all of those persons have their own discipline styles? What do children experience when they move from one adult figure to another and each has his or her own discipline strategy? In a well-functioning village there must be several key roles. One role is that of parent or parents, who ultimately have the final say. Parents have to be the primary decision makers so children know that when a decision is made, it will come from one source. Another role in the village is that of the elders. These elders have the role of providing consultation to the decision makers. They can be consulted at any time on any matter, and parents have to be clear with their children that this consultation process may happen and happen often. There are obviously some "off-limits" areas that parents and children can agree to keep to themselves. These should be negotiated and made clear, but children should have the freedom to negotiate this with parents at any time.

Among the elders, there ought to be different wisdoms present. They have to know the parents as well as the children. They have to have life experience and need a deeper level of knowledge. At least one elder ought to have experience with spirituality and respect for spiritual authority. This individual or group could include a pastor/imam or church leader who can give feedback on how to access one's spiritual power during times of peace and conflict. The elder who has skills in discipline has to be wise in understanding the personalities of children and what strategies are likely to work with different types of kids. This person or group has to be willing to consult parents on when they are losing their concentration, not fulfilling their discipline duties, or are overwhelmed. A discipline elder is not the person you hope will spank your child when you reach the end of your emotional rope. He or she is the one who understands when you are at the end of your emotional rope and will tell you how this is affecting your protection, affection, and correction of your child.

Every parent needs an elder who knows different aspects of the world or who has traversed arenas that parents may or may not have experienced. An elder who has skills in education and academic achievement, and can be a role model for children preparing for the future, is an asset. An elder with special social, musical, or athletic achievement or skills is equally necessary to show parents and children what is available to help them become well-rounded individuals. Finally, an elder who has success in the work world will have skills in navigating those professional obstacles. In many Black families godparents are chosen not only because of their relationships with the parents but also because they bring a different set of talents to the child's world.

Wisdoms That Elders Need to Represent

1. Spiritual wisdom

2. Discipline wisdom

3. Cultural history and community wisdom

4. Academic achievement wisdom

5. Social and athletic achievement wisdom

6. Professional success wisdom

It's important that we find trustworthy persons to parent our children when we are not around. Parenting by ourselves may be necessary. But if it is not, then we have to broker for our children a network, or village, of trusted persons who can add to the love and care that we give—and give us a break! Children benefit from different ways of solving problems, and extended kin (who are related to us by blood and who are not) can support our authority with and nurturance of our children by reinforcing our role and instructions.

The elders can come from family, from the neighborhood, or from activities that children are involved in throughout their lives. The key challenge for parents is developing relationships that last with key elders and making agreements with them about being elders. In Black churches and mosques the ingredients for elder development and village building are already present. The leaders of these establishments have to take a step further and, outside of the church or mosque meeting times, develop CPR agendas that involve the development of local villages with able elders. There are few equivalents to Black religious and spiritual communalism, but we have to take these unique cultural resources to more specific programmatic levels. Our children depend on it. If you don't have a religious affiliation, then there are block captains and neighborhood groups often willing to help in this effort. Don't give up if your first attempts to build a village are rejected.

Although everybody knows that it takes a village to raise a child, no one is giving advice on how to build a village. It takes work to build a village. We strongly recommend that parents watch how their children relate to other adults. Parents can also test out certain adult figures or relatives. How does the child respond? Parents can ask children what they think of the temporary caregiver. There are several strategies to ensure that our children will be safe. But whatever we do, it is important that we introduce our children to adults who add to and support what we are doing.

Our next chapter will focus on how parents begin the village-making and discipline process with newborns and toddlers.

2

Walking the Walk and Talking the Talk of Preschoolers and Toddlers

The egg teaches the hen how to hatch.

Can a parent spoil a three-month-old baby because she holds it too much? I remember coming home with my first baby and trying to figure out why he would start crying every time I put him down. He was changed, fed, and clean. What else did he need? My mother and other people warned me not to hold the baby too much for fear I would spoil him.

One day when one of my friends was visiting, I put the baby down, and sure enough, he started crying. When he started getting louder, my friend asked why I wasn't responding to him. I told her there's nothing wrong with him and what my family said. That is when she gave me a wonderful gift.

She said, "You can never spoil a new baby. He needs to hear your heartbeat, feel your body warmth, and smell you so that he can be at peace. That baby spent nine long months inside you, and everything else outside of you is alien to him. Hold your baby close, tie him on your back while you clean. He knows only you, he needs only you, and it's gonna be that way for a while. And never, never let anyone tell you you're spoiling your child. You, my sister, are mothering him, loving him as God would want you to. Only people you see putting their babies down the hall with a monitor is White folk. You'd better stop copying them people."

Not only did I take that advice, but I noticed many women from all over the world held their babies close to them and nursed them even as *they slept. I also had a very quiet summer that year. My baby and I both slept late a lot of mornings*—together.

Saburah Abdul-Kabir

∽

Remember in Chapter One we told you that parenting is a life-long acquaintance with helplessness? Well, the helplessness starts when your child is born. And this is the best time to begin learning how to manage your frailty.

In African psychology life consists of managing opposites. To learn about and manage your helplessness only makes you stronger as a person and as a parent. Understanding your fears only makes you more courageous. Unfortunately, most of us have been taught about the either-or, not the both-and. We have been taught to run from our fears or find many things to distract us from the challenge of life's opposites. A newborn is God's gift to teach us how to balance our different selves and different experiences as we prepare to raise our child with an equal or greater appreciation of life's different challenges. Simply put, it's the Creator's way of teaching us the both-and.

Discipline in these early years of preschoolers and toddlers covers three areas: (1) Stickin' To—spending quality time with your child to understand more about yourself as you experience the positive and negative feelings and changes of parenting a newborn; (2) Watchin' Over—learning how to protect your child within your home and surrounding community; and (3) Gettin' With—establishing a network of support that can care for your child when you are not around. Let's see how that actually works.

STICKIN' TO: BEING THERE TO UNDERSTAND YOUR UPS AND DOWNS

Discipline for children in this age is 90 percent involvement and availability and 10 percent intervention. In layman's terms, teaching discipline to newborns is more in eye contact, talking back and forth, meeting the child's crying needs, and, mostly, appreciating the joy of watching God's precious gift to you grow. Basically, this first aspect of discipline involves understanding and enjoying *all* of the feelings. So being there is half the battle.

But how can we be there when our children are making the most significant changes in their lives that they will ever make? By not letting anything get in the way of time with our newborn—not work, not family, not friends, not television, not anything. Manage your time so that you get your quality time with your most precious gift. The good thing about this gift is that when you spend time with it, it changes before your eyes, as if you are opening it for the first time, every time.

Discipline in the Early Years

1. *Stickin' To:* Be there to understand the positive and negative changes of parenting.

2. *Watchin' Over:* Protect your young child inside and outside your household.

3. *Gettin' With:* Take action to guarantee good care for your child in your absence.

What to Expect When It's Unpredictable

What can a parent expect from a newborn? Never a dull moment. This is one of the most exciting and fastest moving periods of a child's *and* a parent's life. Too often we see the birth of children from the perspective of the little ones and miss the challenges that parents go through. If we are not there or are busy doing something else, we will miss the changes. And we won't have memories to look back on. A good rule of thumb is that *every baby's action stimulates both an opposite and equal reaction in others*.

Nurturing a newborn seems so easy because who doesn't love a cute little baby, right? (Well, of course there are some people who don't, but we don't want to talk about them.) Babies naturally pull emotions from others just by smiling, by making noises, by just being babies. Discipline begins by structuring your time so that you can enjoy every moment possible and accept every invitation your child gives to you. Babies invite us to be with them most of the time. Parents love this time because they are often wanted by their newborn without any interruptions. (It's when our children get older that they begin to not want us as much.) Attaching yourself to your newborn is essential! And this is as true for fathers as it is for mothers.

Our development as parents mirrors the developmental changes in our children. Saburah Abdul-Kabir calls this "developmental leapfrog"—while parents watch their children change before their eyes, they feel they have to jump and catch up with them. There is also a sadness that comes when your child begins to take on new challenges. Parents often feel like their children are beginning to leave them. We also get sad about losing the comfort of knowing what our child needs at one stage.

Psychologists often discuss adolescence as the stage in which children are beginning to leave the family. But we believe that attachment to parents and learning how to be independent happen from the day they are born and, frankly, never stop. This process of attaching to us and needing to get space from us is probably the most challenging part of the roller-coaster ride we call parenting. So many of us just feel angry and say, "How dare he [or she] grow up and change without my permission or knowledge!"

Howard Stevenson tells about his own mixed emotional struggle with his son's accomplishment of one of his first major developmental tasks:

When Bryan, my son, walked at seven months, I was sad. All the books and my education said that he wouldn't be expected to walk until he was about a year old! I just got used to the idea that when I put him down, he would stay. I also loved the fact that if I held him on top of me, he would stay. The day he walked, I felt great joy watching him tackle a major hurdle, but I also felt sadness because it seemed like he was beginning to walk away from me.

∽

From birth to age three most children learn how to walk, talk, and make sense of their emotions. But, of course, parents have to do the same. What makes it so difficult for you as a parent is that you thought *you* already knew how to walk, talk, and make sense of your emotions. With a newborn you walk differently because you are holding the baby, watching the baby, or following the baby. You do this because you want to keep the baby safe. But expect your walk to change.

Your talk changes too. Babies stimulate loads of interesting behavioral reactions from adults, especially adult relatives. It's not uncommon for the funniest and most frequently recollected moments from babies' young lives to be the ridiculous facial contortions of relatives who could not resist the tempting stares and gurglings of the newborn. When the baby gurgles, we gurgle. When the baby smiles, we smile. When the baby cries, we want to cry. But don't think these parental behaviors are not reactions. They are dependent on the baby and stimulated deep within our souls and personalities. So our souls and personalities change, for a while, when babies come into our lives. It's a gift, too often overlooked and downplayed. Another way we change our talk is that we speak in a special kind of language so that babies and toddlers can understand the world more easily.

When it's time to potty train the toddler, we ask him or her, "Do you have to go potty?" After a million repetitions and without thinking, it is not uncommon for us to tell our spouses, partners, and friends, "First, I have to go to the potty." We call our spouses, partners, and family "Daddy," "Mommy," and "Pop-Pop," but we often forget their first names or the names we used to call them before the newborn came. We used to sleep peacefully, but with a newborn, although sleep is necessary, it is no longer sufficient. We live to watch the baby. These are just some of the many ways we "stick to" our loved ones and that they change our lives.

How Babies Change Adults	
What Babies Do	*What Adults Do*
Babies smile.	We smile.
Babies laugh.	We laugh.
Babies gurgle.	We gurgle.
Babies crawl.	We walk behind them.
Babies know Mommy or Daddy.	We call wives "Mommy" and husbands "Daddy."
Toddlers become potty trained.	We use the language of our children to describe life.

But babies change our emotions too. There are emotions we do not realize are there until they are stimulated by the life of the newborn. Children reveal things about ourselves, our ability to care, our patience, our fears. Oh, yes, our fears. Children open our eyes to see things that were not as possible before. We see the future more because children touch us to protect them now and later on. We see all the things that can bring harm to our most precious gift, and it shakes us. Because we see the harm, we get in touch with our incapacity to prevent it. So yes, we sleep differently. Yes, we walk differently. Yes, we talk differently. But at the heart of these changes is that our feelings are in flux differently.

Love and Fear

Fears come from that untapped capacity to love another human being, something only newborns can ignite. Often the fears of African American parents jump to the future. What if I don't raise him right? What if I'm too strict? What if I'm not strict enough? Will she be able to learn right? What if she is slow?

When your child is born, your life changes literally overnight. The pregnancy is like a trial run for many of the changes families have to face. An important aspect of discipline at this age begins with how families and parents adjust to these sudden changes. So being there is still important, even before the baby comes. Can fathers be there for mothers as mothers go through the pregnancy and the birthing process? Can families be there as parents learn how to parent? Mothers may go through mood shifts, postpartum depression, and confusion because of natural weight gain and hormonal changes in the body. Fathers can also gain weight, have mood swings, and get confused at the number of expectations foisted upon them in such a short period of time. Frankly, to go from being a single couple with the freedom to go to a movie at a moment's notice to becoming a threesome under lockdown in the confines of one's house is sometimes going to feel like prison.

Now, some families adjust by denying the challenges of the newborn. Many of us get so caught up with the wonderment and excitement of a baby that we forget or don't want to know the hardships. Whatever anyone tells you about having your first child, you can't comprehend it until it happens. It's like hurricanes or tornadoes. You can watch them on TV and perhaps you can explain exactly what one is, but until you actually go through it, your knowledge of it is strictly in your head. There is no substitute for the real thing.

Now You Know Them, Now You Don't

As a parent, you often feel like the moment you have this parenting game won, life changes on you, and you are thrown immediately back into a life of perpetual helplessness. Parents who say they have everything under control are either lying or are so rigid that they're missing the boat on other important emotional needs of the child.

He or she who pretends not to be helpless is fooling none of the people, none of the time. You will never know all that you need to know to do the parenting that you imagined. We are always underestimating what it takes to do this job well. Effective parents understand and remind themselves of this all the time. To be an effective parent is to be brave enough to face the helplessness and to be open to help. The first step in knowing oneself is to accept that. One parent says it well:

As soon as I understood them as infants, they became toddlers. As soon as I understood them as toddlers, they became preschoolers. The minute I understood one stage, they had moved on to the next. And then we are at ground zero all over again.

⟀

What is so unique about this developmental period for African American parents? Well, all parents go through the fears and joys of newborns, but African American parents are often overwhelmed about how this child will survive the future of racial hostility.

Special Fears for Black Parents

All Parents' Fears	Black Parents' Fears
Will he be healthy?	If healthy, will he be mistreated?
Will she be successful?	If successful, what price will she have to pay?
Will she be happy?	Will she have to accept less than she deserves?
Will he live a long life?	Will he survive to adulthood?

Recommendations

1. Appreciate your distrust.

2. Ask lots of questions about your child's and family's health.

3. Prepare to teach your child the both-and nature of success in America.

4. Pray for a blessed life, not a long life.

It is the fear of the future that leads us to the next step in discipline—Watchin' Over. It is because we want to protect our children of color who must live in a world that does not appreciate them that parenting young children is unique for African Americans.

WATCHIN' OVER: PROTECTING OUR LITTLE LOVED ONES INSIDE AND OUTSIDE THE HOME

Stickin' To is so important to managing the next level of effective parenting for newborns and toddlers. But it's when we have to protect our helpless loved ones that our natural fight-or-flight stress reactions start to take over. We also learn more about why African American parents are under particular stress compared with other parents. What is it we fear? We fear our helplessness to protect our gift. This is true for all parents, anywhere, anytime. So Stickin' To, or affection, for our newborns and toddlers is so crucial. We shouldn't be scarce in our presence or stingy with our love. But how is this time period unique for African American parents?

African Americans must walk, talk, and feel differently because they are considered to be different Americans. So in addition to the changes of newborns, Black folk will integrate the changes of a lifetime into their parenting. Survival skills, such as distrust of unjust authority for instance, can become a major part of the pregnancy experience. Many Black folk distrust the work of White educated professionals. Physical and behavioral changes in the mother or the fetus can trigger fears for any parent. But the less-than-professional or slow reactions of professionals will always raise the keen eye of African Americans who have experienced racism in health care. The questions raised are, "Am I or my family being treated differently because we are Black?" and "Is my newborn being given the same amount of quality care as any other child?" For some, however, the hospital and health care system raises more helplessness because it is a system we have been taught to simply listen to and not talk back to.

Black Survival Skills That Make Parenting Newborns Different

Black Survival Skills

1. Distrust of educated White professionals

2. Withholding of feelings from professionals

3. Distrust of advice from parenting books

Recommendations

1. Ask lots of questions and find professionals of color.

2. Share your emotions.

3. Find culturally relevant books and materials.

Our fear of being discriminated against raises all kinds of traumatic memories and pain. Sometimes it's overwhelming. But we'll give you ways to manage this pain a little later. Just remember that your toddler or newborn needs a clear-headed parent looking out for him or her.

Unique Struggles of Parenting Newborns for Black Men

Unfortunately, our societal views of men do not help us help fathers during this crucial stage. Many Black men are struggling with meeting the demands of a narrow definition of manhood that suggests men are emotionless, distant, and unable to contribute anything meaningful in the way of physical affection or managing the daily care of young children. That definition also includes views that men are breadwinners and that making money is more important than spending time with their children. But when Black men take the risk of moving outside society's narrow definitions of manhood, they grow in unimaginable ways.

We encourage Black men very simply during this stage. If you want to lose the power and influence over your children that men like to have in life in general, then don't spend time with your newborn. If you want to be a fumbling, bumbling, have-no-say, brain-dead dad when it comes to the affairs of your child's life, then don't spend time with your newborn. If you want to have mothers and others making more decisions about your children than you, then don't spend time with your newborn.

The only way to know your child is to be there, during everything and doing everything. Change the diapers so you can see and know the relief in your child's disposition when such a change is made. Give him or her the bath so that you feel the softness of the skin and watch how the baby responds to touch. Hold him or her and rock him or her to sleep as often in a day as you can so that you can feel the power of cooing and singing and no one has to tell you what it's like. Feel the helplessness now so that you can learn how to influence your child in the future. If men want the "power" of fatherhood, they have to experience the helplessness of parenting from the cradle to the grave.

The men who haven't experienced this "power rush" have all kinds of thoughts that prevent them from risking being involved. These thoughts range from buying into society's narrow definition of manhood to trying to keep distance from anything that remotely looks like mothering.

Thoughts Black Men Have As They Struggle with Being Men and Fathers

"Real men don't have emotions."

"Real men don't go to pregnancy checkups or baby doctor visits."

"Real men don't have questions about newborns or how to raise
   Black children."

"Real men don't change diapers."

"Real men don't get scared."

"Real men don't cook, clean, or handle cleaning supplies."

"Real men don't get scared that their children won't reach their
   potential."

"Real men don't baby-sit, give baths, or make 'goo-goo' sounds
   to babies."

"Real men don't hold soft cuddly babies for too long."

"Real men could drop little babies."

"Real men find women who take care of their children."

Now, all of these thoughts are incorrect in our thinking, and the
opposites are true. But the real issue is that these are temporary and
can best be challenged by investment in the child's life.

The biggest challenge of fatherhood for Black men is accepting
the enormousness of the role of protection and Watchin' Over. Being a father of a child of African American or biracial descent is an
amazing reality because the responsibilities of one's life change. The
reason that fathers have to use these early years as intense training
is because without these lessons, one will find it very hard to manage the lessons of the future. The primary goal of the first few years
is knowing your children, and you can't know your children fully if
you don't participate in most of the experiences they have. Children wet and soil their diapers. That's an experience, isn't it? That's
a lesson, isn't it? Be there for it. Why? Because you can watch how
babies are relieved from the changing of a diaper. You can understand that some cries that babies give are about discomfort, others
are about needing attention, and others are about hunger. If you are
not there, you can't know your child.

Why is knowing your child so important? It's not just so you can
have the skills to handle the future or so you can be Superparent,
managing problems with a single word. No. It's also because chil-

dren teach us about ourselves like no other person can. There is no other relationship that teaches us more about ourselves than our relationship with our children. If you don't know your child, you may miss out on opportunities to know yourself. So no other relationship can pull or push at us like our relationship with our children. No other relationship can reveal the gaps in our life, holes in our heart, and fears in our mind like our relationship with our children.

One major reason children are a gift from God is that by revealing parts of ourselves that no one else can, they help us grow in ways not possible without them. This is not a statement about whether someone should have children. It's a statement that if you have children, you should spend time with them, and it will affect you as much as it will affect them.

Why Children Are a Gift from God

1. There is no other relationship like the parent-child relationship, so nothing can replace it.

2. Children reveal empty areas in our lives that can be addressed.

3. Children pull emotions from us that teach us about ourselves.

4. Children, unlike adults, are not slaves to the problems of the world.

5. Children will say things we are too afraid to hear from others.

6. By loving us, they see more of who we are than who we want to be.

Challenges of Physical Discipline for Young Children

As we watch over our children, we will undoubtedly struggle with whether or not to use physical discipline. Many parents find it hard to handle children who act up because it makes them feel out of control. African Americans have been criticized publicly for being inferior on many levels, and the area of parenting is not exempt. So it makes perfect sense that many Black parents would raise children from very young ages with this in mind.

For many African American parents, public humiliation by a child is seen as the worst that can happen. This is not only because such humiliation suggests that we don't know how to parent. The humiliation may trigger those same feelings of Black inferiority that suggest "Black people don't know what they are doing." So spoiled children become the representation of failed parenting and heightened Black inferiority. Parents who have grown up with physical discipline in their childhood will struggle a lot about how, when, and whether to use spanking.

I can't stand no spoiled children. If a child is spoiled, he better not be around me, because I will tear his little butt up!

Darryl, age forty-nine, father of three and grandfather

☙

Another reason why parents will bristle at children who are unruly has to do with the negative feelings that these children stimulate. Children can stimulate positive feelings in us, but they can also trigger feelings of intense anger. As adults, we have often come to expect the predictable and the routine. In fact, we expect routine in the most basic of daily tasks. But young children and toddlers not only make routine unpredictable, but they do it in a way that disrupts the professional and personal lives of adults. So it's like having your life messed up without your permission *and* not being allowed to scream about it. So anger builds up, especially for the obsessive, need-to-have-everything-in-its-right-place adult! Where does this anger go? Well, if we aren't careful, it can work its way back to our children when we say "No!" or "Stop!" with hostility.

Another belief that some parents have is that if you start early, you can stamp out rebellion in children. In America the children most vulnerable to child abuse are those age five and younger. Most child deaths happen in this age bracket as well. Why? Well, some researchers believe it's because the children are so small and can't defend themselves. Others believe that it's because parents are inexperienced when their children are that age and make considerable mistakes. We believe it's a combination of these issues.

Children stimulate emotions in us that we are unprepared for and that are unmatched in the history of relationships during our lifetime. Sometimes physical retribution is a reaction to what children stimulate in us. The cry of a young child is more piercing than the sonic boom of a jet flying overhead or than the screeching of fingernails on a blackboard. It sinks into the soul and psyche of the parent and brings memories and experiences long forgotten back from the dead. So we have to be careful not to translate our reactions into physical expressions.

Understanding that we have feelings of anger toward our children is essential to managing those feelings. African American parents who are undergoing the exceptional pressures of their lives in addition to the intense experience of having a newborn will have their stress management strategies put to the test. Sometimes, using physical discipline comes from not having effectively managed the different stressors in one's life, which can lead to regret or remorse at our actions.

I spanked my two-year-old the other day for pulling down all the laundry on top of the counter after I told her not to crawl up on the sofa and reach. Do you know how long it took me to fold them clothes! Wouldn't you know it—as soon as I was out of eyesight, she did it again! She made me so mad! That child is gonna break her neck one of these days, or I'll do it first.

Sarah, age twenty-two, Philadelphia

So what can African American parents do when this kind of stress might take over? We do *not* recommend the use of physical discipline, but we want to give information to explain why some people do. Our goal is to help parents who use it stop or reduce its use so that they know enough to apply what's in the best interest of the child.

A key reason for the use of spanking is the parental challenge of meeting the demand of Watchin' Over. Most parents who use physical discipline do so out of a desire to maximize the protection of their children. It's like a way to imprint on children's memory a lesson they won't forget when parents are not around. Or so they think. Although children may remember the spanking, they often forget the lesson parents are trying to communicate. In fact, parents are often not sure what lesson they are trying to give when they spank. This confusion can only lead to hostility in children, more helplessness in parents, and less secure protection of the child. This leads us to consider the last aspect of discipline, Gettin' With. This aspect involves correction, but the kind of correction that increases the chances that our young children will be safe and will remember the lessons we want them to keep inside when we are not around.

GETTIN' WITH: TAKING ACTION TO PROTECT AND LOVE OUR LITTLE ONES

At this stage of your child's life, correction involves preparation and taking action beyond any form of conventional discipline. It's about establishing a context of safety so your children will be cared for when you are not around. Unfortunately, when parents are unprepared, the mistakes they make become larger. This is where a lot of parents regret the use of spanking, for example, because in their hearts they realize that maybe the spanking wasn't about the child but, rather, about their own sense of helplessness. Mistakes are to be expected, so get used to it. But preparation for potential challenges can ease the road. This is why Gettin' With is about taking charge of our fears, applying action strategies to combat our feelings of helplessness, and refusing to sit back and watch our young children grow up defenseless.

Parents of African American infants and toddlers often have several questions related to establishing a context of safety for their children.

Frequently Asked Questions

- What should I do about my racial distrust of medical and health professionals?

- Is there more to discipline than what I do with my child?

- How can I use discipline as both what I do when my child is behaving and what I do when he is misbehaving?

- What should I expect to see in my child when discipline works well?

- What should I do about the fears I have for my newborn's future concerning the struggles of being African American?

Our responses to these questions can be summed up in ten recommendations.

1. *Panic, but not for long.* One thing you can say about panic is that at least it's a recognition of one's helplessness. So it does serve one purpose. Often panic is a way to relieve stress but allow yourself only so much time to wig out. Expect it, but don't wallow in it. Panic becomes therapeutic once you allow it a little time but recognize it as nonproductive. Remember, self-knowledge is the highest form of knowledge, so knowing when and how you panic is the first step to managing it and coming up with helpful, clear-headed

decisions. Often African Americans panic over the pain and frustration of being discriminated against. We panic even more when we consider our loved ones may not get what they deserve. By managing these fears, we can manage the situation and walk away feeling good about being effective problem solvers, feeling good about being role models for our loved ones, and feeling great about protecting our family effectively.

2. *Talk out your fears, but then evaluate what you learn.* The greatest cost or tragedy of any emotional experience (positive or negative) is not to fully understand it. By talking out your fears to someone you care about and who cares about you, you can reduce half of the anxiety that comes with fears you cannot resolve immediately. Studies have shown that many African Americans suffer from hypertension due to the suppression of anger related to racism and discrimination. To swallow this anger will have a life-threatening influence on one's physical health. After talking out your fears and examining what you've learned from the self-expression, make decisions.

3. *Recognize that some of your fears are for the future, not the present.* Your newborn needs you now. You have a lot to learn before some fears become real. Watching her grow will give you the knowledge you need to resolve future conflicts or challenges. After talking out the fears, you will realize what is reasonable to manage now and what is best to hold off managing until later.

4. *Appreciate your distrust.* Stickin' To means we have to stick to our own feelings that we have learned over the years as people of color in America. Trust your gut about discrimination and gather as much information as you can about your distrust. Is there a vibe that lets you know someone is trying to devalue or disrespect you because you are different? Is it consistent? Are there behaviors that match the emotions you are picking up? By thoughtfully evaluating the situation, you are better able to make the best decisions on whether to challenge the racism you see, move on beyond it, or whatever. The fact that you can make a decision about the insult will lead to your improved psychological health.

5. *Ask lots of questions about your concerns to medical professionals*. Our second recommendation to parents during and after pregnancy was to *ask, ask, ask!* Ask lots of questions, no matter how small or silly you think the question is. In the case of health care, the rule that "the squeakiest wheel gets the grease" applies 99.9 percent of the time. So squeak! It is not possible to protect your child or your family when you don't have adequate information. If all you are worried about is looking stupid, remember that the saying "There is no such thing as a stupid question" is very true. So even if it feels stupid, ask it anyway. Even if someone looks at you funny, ask anyway. This is your baby, and no one has to raise him but you and your family. It's better to know and look stupid than to be stupid and not know. And if you are not satisfied with your present medical or health professional, find professionals of color who can help you understand your experience as an African American. Finding reading materials about African American health issues for children is also essential. At the end of this book, there is a resource section containing suggested reading materials for parents of African American youth.

But whatever you do, don't be afraid to confront professionals. They have the duty to explain everything until you understand it and to treat you and your loved ones fairly. Demand it. A famous Caribbean psychiatrist, Franz Fanon, has a wonderful quote that applies here: "I have one right and one duty alone—to demand right behavior from the other. And not to renounce my freedom through my choices" (Fanon, 1962, p. 132). If we choose to stand up for ourselves and our loved ones, then racial discrimination cannot have a hold on our mental health. Studies on racism have shown that those African American adults who experience discrimination but do nothing to object to it are more likely to suffer physical and mental health problems.

6. *Prepare to teach your child about how being Black is a both-and experience*. We will talk about this throughout the book, but African American parents must know how to talk to their children about race from age three to age thirty-three. Why? We believe it's because the

reality and psychology of racism and discrimination in America have not changed over the centuries.

The psychological consequence of racism and psychological enslavement is the same today as it was in 1700—the trauma of feeling inferior. The way you manage this unique stress when your children are very young will help you help them manage it as they get older. So choose interactive reading and play materials and toys for your children that may accentuate their cultural background while helping them manage the weird vibes they may experience from others. By teaching young children to appreciate their feelings, we are helping them to manage the hostility of others.

But don't forget your own experiences. Don't shut them out. Talking to toddlers about racism doesn't have to be a college history lesson. Tell them about people who are confused and whose biggest problem is that they think they are better than other people who are brown or yellow or dark skinned. Tell them that you want them to grow up to appreciate all of God's children and that to think you are better is not following what God has planned because only God can claim to be better than any one of us. Racism and the key elements of inferiority and superiority can be addressed and challenged, albeit differently, in each developmental period, from the time your children are able to speak and understand good and bad until they are adolescents.

7. *Spend most of your energy on your child.* Too often we put out so much energy to tear down the walls of society and injustice that we forget our loved ones. Unfortunately, one area where this is most prevalent is with the children of leaders or ministers. Some parents are more equipped to fight than stay home. If you are going to expend energy, spend most of it on the child, not the ones who commit the injustice.

Young children need to know that their parents will protect them from discrimination but not at the expense of losing a parent's affection. Spend time with the child explaining, nurturing, and answering their questions so they can be better prepared for the future. And yes, starting with toddlers is the best way to learn how to do this.

8. *Know what infants and toddlers do!* Knowing that infants will have different types of cries can save you lots of heartache and worry. Knowing that two- and three-year-olds can say "No" strongly is a very important piece of information. Some folks call this stage the "terrible twos," but that's only from the perspective of overwhelmed, unprepared parents. If hearing your child say "No" loudly with such vigor, and thinking that he is acting twenty-two instead of two, is very hard to tolerate, don't get discouraged. This is where children are learning to imitate your own behavior. Consider this.

What did you do and say mostly to your child from the ages of one to two? We know that most children start moving and crawling at four to six months and walking around one year, right? Well, when children become mobile, so do parents. You follow your child to protect them, right? Well, what do you say when you are following them? "Johnny, wait. Good. Stop! No, don't touch! Good, baby. Hold—hold it. Good—thank you for giving me—wait, no! Don't—yes, good—no, wait—good job, baby!" So we may often teach our children how to be obstinate. But this is a normal part of learning how to manage the world at two years old.

A Different Look at the Terrible Twos

When parents stick to, watch over, and get with children from birth to age two, they follow their children more than any other time in their life. They are interested in watching them smile and do new things as well as protecting them from danger. When children start to move, crawl, and walk, it changes how we speak. We often speak in short sentences, loudly, and we repeat ourselves a lot. So it's not uncommon for adults of one- to two-year-olds to walk behind children as they learn to walk and explore the world. As we follow them, we are often telling them not to do things that might be dangerous, while at the same time encouraging them to try new stuff.

So the conversation may sound like this:

(Latifah, fifteen months old, also known as Tee-Tee, pulls herself up, stands up and looks around, stares at adults in the room, and laughs and smiles like she owns the world.)

MOTHER: Latifah, go girl! Look at you!

(Tee-Tee moves toward the kitchen.)

MOTHER: Tee-Tee, where you going, child?

(Adults laugh at Tee-Tee's assertiveness.)

MOTHER: Tee-Tee, Mommy doesn't—

(Tee-Tee starts sprinting toward the stove, where baking is going on.)

MOTHER: Tee-Tee, wait. Hold up child. Child—no—don't touch.

(Tee-Tee, looking up at her mother, who finally catches up with her, says with her eyes, "What?")

MOTHER: No, stove hot. Hot, no!

(Tee-Tee laughs and makes a beeline to the trash can in the kitchen and starts to stick her hand in the pail. Her relatives are laughing, but now they are laughing at Tee-Tee's mother because of all the times she pretended to know what she was doing and talked about how easy parenting would be.)

MOTHER: Tee—no, don't—stop! Come here, child. No, no, no. Mommy doesn't want you to get your hands dirty.

(Tee-Tee's mother picks her up and carries her back to the living room, where the adults are, while Tee-Tee simultaneously smiles and stares at her mom. After about ten minutes of distraction, hugging, kissing, and holding from the adults, Tee-Tee looks into the kitchen, and this scenario starts all over again, with little twists along the way. For example, she goes into the refrigerator or under the sink, where pots and pans are, or near prepared food.)

Now, imagine this happening every day for a year or more, and then tell us what children should be doing at twenty-four, twenty-seven, or thirty months old.

The most significant language that this parent has shared with Tee-Tee consists of "No!" and "Stop!" So Tee-Tee knows that there is power in the word *no,* especially if you say it loud, because parents follow you, the big people laugh, the wrinkles in Mom's face make funny changes, and everything stops. At the same time, Tee-Tee is learning to speak. Children's language development is most pronounced from two and a half to three and a half years old. So when children become two, they learn that they can put all this power together in one word: *no.* Children are always learning, even if it makes parents nuts.

Why do children at two or three say "No" a lot?
Because they are learning to be their own person, and we
teach them that it is very powerful to say "No."

---

9. *Get help.* No man or woman is an island. Always ask for help with a task that was meant for a village. Yes, it takes a village to raise a child, but what does it take to raise a village? It takes gettin' with family and friends to be the village you need when you have nearly lost your mind. Parents who take on village tasks by themselves should expect to get overwhelmed. Avoid the use of physical discipline because too often the message of love and caring gets confused

with fear and helplessness. We don't know any parent who wants to communicate fear and helplessness to their child. Getting help communicates to your young child that you *do* know how to manage tough situations.

10. *Pray.* Pray for help with the emotions that arise from being African American and being treated unfairly. Our reliance on the Creator or our religious and spiritual resources can not only reduce stress but can help us problem-solve in ways that we had not thought possible. Prayer is absolutely essential at all times, but it is especially helpful when we fear the worst.

Why? Because prayer means you are relying on a divine source that is higher than yourself, greater than your fears, and who can see the future in ways you cannot. Psychologically, giving the burden to your Creator allows you to reduce worry about things you have no control over anyway. Anxiety is reduced, and you have more feeling and thinking resources to make the best decisions to love your child. Having your little child (of course, they are always little children to us) in danger of being discriminated against raises the most out-of-control feelings, but prayer can help you manage them.

These ten recommendations are just a few that we will cover in this book.

In this chapter we focused on parents of infants and newborns. Now, we know it doesn't matter how old our kids get. *We* always think of them as our little ones. But in the next chapter we will talk about the early-school-age little ones from four to nine years old. They have different lives and different experiences, and they need parents to treat them differently, even if they are still little to us.

To summarize, the discipline of very young children is about nurturing, structuring and spending time, and taking action on behalf of your defenseless loved ones. Avoid physical discipline. Parents who discipline with love, close supervision, and quality time will know what manages their children's emotions and won't need a lot of dramatic physical discipline. By Gettin' With, or taking action on the societal barriers that interfere with our children's receiving adequate health care and opportunities to appreciate themselves, parents can feel less helpless and have more emotional resources to spend on their little ones. It's on the little ones that it needs to be spent the most. Remember, being a parent is more than a biological commitment—it's a life commitment, and anybody can be a donor. During this stage the love connection is so important. As the African proverb states, "Even though you may enter the house, you don't always enter the hearts." For us, parenting infants and toddlers is the time for parents to enter the hearts.

3

When Black Children Are Cute, the World Is Watching

Discipline and Elementary School–Age Children

Instruction in youth is like engraving in stone.

For us, Stickin' To for four- to eleven-year-olds involves managing and negotiating how to emotionally support children in a way that fits their developmental needs. It's about how we get permission from our children to show them love and affection in a racially hostile world. Watchin' Over involves supervising our children's exposure to the world's insensitivity and attending to the events they are involved in. Gettin' With involves teaching them to respect structure and limits and how to reflect on the meaning of those limits without losing their voice in the process.

STICKIN' TO: GETTING PERMISSION TO HUG YOUR CHILD WHEN NO ONE ELSE WILL

So I walked my six-year-old to his school. We hold hands as we go. The closer we got to the school, I noticed he wanted to fix his coat and let go of my hand in the process. We came to the school's front door. As I usually do, I bent over, ready to kiss and hug him, and before I knew it, he turned his cheek. And then he said, "Daaaad," in a low whisper so that no one but I could hear it. I was shocked. I didn't know what to do. I just kind of looked around, hoping no one saw.

❧

Hoping No One Saw

Facing the harsh reality that our children are changing is easier when they are infants and toddlers. Although difficult to manage, moving from a crawling baby to a walking baby is not the same as your child wanting you to stop hugging him. Brace yourself, parents. When children get verbal, all bets are off. They can tell us stuff. They can choose. And sometimes they don't choose us. Or at least it feels that way. Between the ages of four and eleven, children will become social beings, and—once again—our lives will change forever.

At this stage parents are beginning to learn that giving hugs and kisses is not as easy as it was the first few years. And it's embarrassing. As infants, our children were immobile and wanted more affection with every touch. As they grow, children begin to explore the world on their own and want their parents to be less involved in their explorations. Children at this age are learning to be concerned about what the world thinks of them. This world begins to include same-age kids and new authority figures, like teachers and relatives.

During ages four to eleven of a child's life, he or she must engage in multiple social relationships for the first time, and the biggest job he or she has is to do well with others. The child must manage school, which is not a small task, given the many relationships there: teachers, principals, crossing guards, bus drivers, cafeteria workers, nurses, new kids and their parents, kids they know, kids they don't know, bus-riding kids, neighborhood kids, older kids, and school kids. As kids negotiate these different people and their different demands, they get stressed—really stressed.

Studies have shown that many poor urban Black youth experience depression at a greater rate than most other children if they see or endure the tragedy of various expressions of urban violence. For some kids, getting into trouble is a way to mask the sadness and stress of managing the world's multiple demands. Moreover, middle- and upper-class Black youth are not exempt: suicide has increased dramatically in the last decade among these groups. Although the percentages of Black child and adolescent suicide are still low compared with those of White youth, it is worthy of note. Some have attributed this increase to a sense of cultural alienation from one's place in the world that materialism or faith in material goods (having the latest fashion, toy, or commodity on the market as a way to define your identity) cannot remedy. We say all this to say that Black children need as much Stickin' To as they can get, and from as many different caring adults as possible, regardless of their social status.

So how do we show our affection in these situations? Well, we can *ask* them how they want to be hugged and kissed. They really don't want you to stop. They just want to be a little more in control of when you hug and kiss and who can watch it. You can make demands too, now. Don't be a passive parent in this regard. Tell your child or children that you have to have at least seventeen hugs and a hundred kisses a day but that you are willing to concede that they occur in the car, on the way to school, once they get home, and before bedtime—all out of the sight of other children who would think he or she is a big baby.

Hoping Others See Him as a Star

These issues are no different for any parent. Yet during the ages of four to eleven, Black parents have to consider these normal developmental changes plus the cultural implications of how our children look to the rest of the world. Stickin' To, or affection, for Black youth includes all of the challenging issues we've mentioned, but it also includes understanding how Black youth may not be nurtured by others. This perspective of being unloved by the rest of the world is a fear that may be more or less justified.

Some basic fears still preoccupy the minds of many African American parents: Will my child be treated fairly? Will she receive her due recognition? Will authority figures interpret her behavior accurately? Will the authority figures see her intelligence, her skill, her potential? Will they distrust him because he is Black? What do I have to do extra to compensate for the world's distrust of my child?

This fear is compounded when we consider how, during the ages of four to eleven, our child is leaving us for the first time. Not only must they negotiate new relationships, but so must we. Not only must they learn new things about the world, but we also must learn new things about them as they grow. So Stickin' To also relates to our needing to stay close enough to our children in order to know how the world shapes them—and who they are becoming.

We have to check out the parents of the friends. We have to make time for our children to enjoy these new relationships. And most of all, we have to go to lots of birthday parties at Chuck E. Cheese or Pizza Hut or Discovery Zone or wherever there's an arcade, some pizza, and a big fluffy rat or rabbit that wants to congratulate the birthday child.

So we have to give our children what some teachers hold back. We have to give affection in abundant supply to make up for when others who should give it don't. We have to reframe the insults of other children and the nasty looks of not-so-caring adults. We have to love them in ways that others will not because they only see race or inferiority when they look at our child. We want our children to leave conflictual situations with adults, with the question, "What's wrong with that person that they would treat me this way?" instead of "What's wrong with me that causes people to treat me like this?"

This brings up a number of parental struggles in the area of nurturance for many Black folk. But the one that is perhaps key is how not to raise a spoiled child.

⟪∽⟫

A child without correction is like a river without a bank.

⟪∽⟫

Tough Love or Bluff Love: What Is a Spoiled Kid?

When children don't feel safe, they often react in ways that keep them isolated. What about the child who throws temper tantrums in public? What about the child described as "spoiled"? Usually when Black folk use the word *spoiled*, they mean a child who controls his parents and blindly tries to manage life on his own. Behaviorally, it looks like a child who wants his own way and will do anything to get it. A child who feels that screaming and resisting are the best ways to get what he wants is often a child who does not feel secure at all. If this were the image of "spoiled," then a lot of parents would agree that this will not lead to positive mental and social health for the "spoiled" child.

Often, "spoiled" children don't feel safe because they are not sure where their personal boundaries are. This clarity about limits is key to helping children define themselves. Without clear boundaries, children may feel a false sense of freedom that can be overwhelming. It's like having a birthday party but being the only child to show up; or like having a birthday party and fearing the fluffy rat or rabbit will forget to congratulate you; or like having a birthday party and knowing everyone is only coming for the fluffy rodent and not you. The child feels like she has attention but that it's empty attention.

Children feel safe when they know what to expect from parents. Confusing expectations cause anxiety. Often misbehavior is a way parents can tell that their rules are not clear. When children feel safe, they want to please their parents and to engage in behaviors that increase that feeling of safety.

Why discipline your child? One primary reason for discipline is to help your child feel safe. Parenting African American children and youth is a challenging task in a world of increasing hostility and intolerance, a world that is not safe. Black parents have to balance their own life struggles with raising children to be healthy, wise, and safe, often at great personal sacrifice. Disciplining children is one of the most challenging aspects of parenting—perhaps the most difficult—because it takes time. And too often single parents, hardworking parents, and stressed-out parents find time as valuable as money. So the last thing a parent wants to deal with is a child who adds more stress by being overly needy. But that is also no reason to withhold the setting of limits from children.

If we don't examine how we discipline our children, then someone else will surely jump at the chance to control him or her. More money is being spent on the building of prisons than educational institutions in our society. Increasingly, children are being tried as adults in criminal cases, so there is societal lack of caring for children, both financially and emotionally. With the continued negative stereotyping and racism against African American youth, the tendency to control the perceived excessive behavior of these youth warrants cultural hypervigilance on the part of parents of color. There is no shortage of societal systems ready to pounce on, diagnose, and incarcerate unruly Black children. But we must balance our protection against racism with teaching our children the will to love themselves.

∽

> *He who is not chastised by his parents is chastised by his ill-wisher.*

∽

"You Better Not Cry"

No effective discipline strategy is complete without some serious, consistent emotional nurturing. To know your child is to know what he likes and doesn't like, what she fears and what she doesn't fear, what makes her happy and what makes her sad. So parents have to prepare themselves and make themselves available for when their children begin to lose control of their emotions without warning.

We believe—no, we *know*—that you can't give a child too much affection. It's not possible. But what parents often fail to do is set up a structure that allows kids to feel safe as they are being loved.

Remember, if a child doesn't feel safe, he or she gets distracted and can't see the love as easily. The following lists give parents guidelines on what being spoiled does and does not mean.

A child is spoiled when

1. The child wants his or her way regardless of the circumstances and expects that adults are there to jump at his bidding

2. The child tells the parents what to do all of the time by whining

3. The parents are afraid to establish guidelines and consequences for misbehaving

4. The child feels insecure because there is no structure in his life to protect him and so has to take matters into his own hands

It does not mean a child is spoiled when

1. The child is asking to get her basic needs met

2. The child cries

3. The child breaks things accidentally

4. The child is afraid

5. The child wants parents to cuddle him

6. The parents feel like they have given too much to their child

7. The child disagrees with parents on some matters

8. The child shares her opinions forcefully

But if you believe that "spoiled" means any child who causes parents stress, then it's likely that you are without the support necessary to parent effectively. Children will always bring parents to the brink of having their own temper tantrums. (We talk a lot about children's temper tantrums but forget that parents have them too.) Spoiled does not mean children who ask to have their needs met, who cry, who want parental feedback and guidance, who are loud every now and then, who play until they go too far, who sometimes break things.

Too often, when parents are overwhelmed, normal childhood behavior gets categorized as "spoiled" because parents feel like their own needs are not being met. Giving emotional, mushy, kiss-you-in-the-face, touchy-feely love is not spoiling your child. And children in the elementary school years need it as much as infants and cute, cuddly toddlers. Four- to eleven-year-olds just may ask for it differently. If you see "spoiled" behavior, your first mission, should you choose to accept it, is to make your child feel safer. How? By setting clear limits that he or she knows you will set almost every time he or she disobeys or needs to understand how his or her behavior affects others. *Black parenting that is focused solely on structure and behavior can sometimes miss the mark if it does not shift in tone and attention to give children time and space to cry, laugh, and react naturally—in the parent's presence, with the child's permission, with the parent watching.*

WATCHIN' OVER: SUPERVISING THE CULTURAL EXPERIENCES OF OUR YOUNG CHILDREN

A child is in the supermarket, and the parent doesn't want any trouble. So she may give her child that same lecture many Black parents give their children outside of the store: "Don't ask for nothin', don't touch nothin', don't look at nothin'. If I didn't give it to you, it ain't yours! Don't be actin' like those White kids. I don't care how many you see actin' like a park ape—you don't!"

❧

Because the World Is Watching

Sometimes when Black parents use discipline, they do so out of a keen awareness or a gut-level feeling of how racism plays out in the world. This discipline is based on their direct experience or observation that the margin of error for Black children is smaller than for Whites or others.

When children are five and six, they begin to transact with the world to get their wants met. It's during this stage that they begin to interact with others in the world. It's during this stage that they will want what all children want—to be able to enjoy the things they see and hear. They also realize that parents are the ones who get things for them, and they will ask, ask, and ask their parents, sometimes until their parents give in out of exhaustion.

White people let their kids talk to them any which way. I can't see it. If my child embarrasses me in public, people gonna think I don't know what I'm doing. No, not gonna happen in this life. If my child so much as rolls her eyes, she knows that she will get it. That's a sign of disrespect, and I will not have my child disrespecting me. 'Cause when she gets older, she ain't gonna respect other adults, and they'll see her as a troublemaker, and she won't get anywhere in life.

∽

So here we are once again—at our place of fears and helplessness. It's just a new level of fear and a different type of helplessness. When our children were infants, we couldn't wait until they spoke their first words. We worried that they wouldn't reach their milestones as quickly as they were supposed to. We learned to get over that fear by holding the child, understanding and knowing the child, and loving the child. Now our fears switch because we realize we are venturing into uncharted territory. Now they talk incessantly—so much so, it is hard to stop them from talking and wanting and telling us what they want. Now that children can talk, we fear they may say or do things that the rest of the world is ready to pounce on.

What Black parents of four- to eleven-year-olds are worried about is absolutely normal, but sometimes it is based on the fear that if their children act up in public, their parenting will be questioned. And there is the additional fear that bad Black parenting is worse than any other form of bad parenting. Most Black parents don't want to hear anyone say anything bad about their children. Moreover, they fear that their children will be perceived and labeled as criminal and out of control, despite the fact that White children can climb to the top of the aisle racks in a store and swing from aisle to aisle and everyone will consider this developmentally appropriate.

The "park ape" reference is not coincidental. Many African Americans have to struggle through the images of being perceived as animals. Frankly, children in our society from all ethnic and racial backgrounds are often talked about as animals—"little monkeys" for example. But the reference to African American children as animalistic does not go away when they stop being cute little babies. It intensifies as they grow to become prepubescent and adolescent youth and the world sees them as "menaces to society." It seems to stay with them. Society does not make the transition. So parents will do all that they can to keep their children from walking into the stereotypes.

Walking into Stereotypes

Once someone perceives you as ineffective, the label "bad" feels permanent. And so there is a lot of energy spent to never let White people see you sweat. The more you try to explain it, the more inferior you begin to sound.

A major fear of parenting children from four to eleven is walking into the stereotypes. It's like walking into the street in front of an oncoming vehicle. All parents have this fear, right? You have that dream where you are doing all you can to protect your child. You hold their hands and look both ways, and you beg your children to hold your hand and look both ways.

At this age children begin to venture out more independently. They want a little more space from you. They want you far enough away that you can be seen but not heard. (Ironic, isn't it? There are some parents who want the same from their children at this age.) Between ages four and eleven your child will want you to stop hugging him in public, stop treating her like a little child, and stop worrying so much.

So you tell them a million times over, "Make sure you look both ways before you cross the street!" And this verbal child tells you, "Ye-e-e-s, Mommm!" or "Ye-e-e-s, Daaad!" as if you were punishing her every time you start a sentence with the phrase "Make sure . . . ."

But with all that reminding and with their growing independence, you still fear the worst can happen. You still fear your child will be preoccupied with child things or playing with a friend or just being happy enough not to worry that anything can happen to him or her. It's this fear that rises up in us despite all our efforts to protect our children, that leads to more sleepless nights. Parents can't easily shake these nightmares of not being there for their child all the time.

Well, the fear of walking into the stereotypes is the same. You want your child to understand the complexity of racism. But he or she is too young to fully comprehend it, so you do the next best thing. You harp, nag, and remind over and over again to "be good" because what you really want is for them not to behave in such a way that the world or White people or even family and friends will misdiagnose him or her as a "park ape."

As we have said in previous chapters about fears and helplessness being a both-and situation, there is a both-and challenge to parenting elementary school children. The benefit of this walking-into-the-stereotypes fear is that it could prepare parents to establish cultural enrichment experiences so that their children learn how to reject majority culture's tendency to see them as inferior. The tragedy of the walking-into-the-stereotypes fear is that parents can become so preoccupied with it that they subtly teach their children that being afraid of what others think is more important than knowing and appreciating your cultural self.

Can Black Parents Raise Children to Be Afraid of Whites?

If Black parents parent with White racism in mind but do not communicate what this means at the child's developmental level of understanding, they may be teaching the theme of inferiority in their parenting. The key message children of color might benefit from most is one of liberation and healing. Eventually, parents must tell their children *why* they don't want them to act crazy in the supermarkets, *why* they have to behave differently than White children, and *why* this will seem unfair. Of course, not all White children behave in an unruly fashion, but the perception is quite prominent among many African American parents because of cultural parenting style differences.

Children don't understand racism the way adults do. Yet sometimes adults forget they are surviving racism, and we don't always question why we must survive. We assume that fighting racism is just living. So we don't consider how we may communicate that Black inferiority is at the bottom of all of this survival. The trouble with a subtle acceptance of the theme that "Blacks are less than" is the tacit acceptance of the theme that "Whites are better than." In an either-or worldview, the opposite is always lurking in the background. So fear of White "superiority" is often what children and adults learn when cultural pride in Black talent is not accurately emphasized or when Black inferiority themes are not accurately challenged and reframed.

African Americans are traumatized daily by being perceived as inferior, but we often don't consider it trauma. We consider it "the way life is," and sometimes we expect our children to just live through it as we and so many other sons and daughters of enslaved Africans have done. Unfortunately, by not telling our children about the craziness of the context and focusing primarily on our behavior in it, we are unconsciously blaming the victim. Unfortunately, what children learn from these experiences is to swallow one's anger, to underappreciate one's racial pain, and to minimize the potency of one's difference.

The remedy is for parents to try and balance conversation about racial oppression with cultural pride. The greatest cultural value a parent of color can give to his or her child is the value that the child is a cultural being and is loved and lovable; this includes encouraging the child not to accept another person's view that would contradict this fact. So being afraid of the oppression is accepting that the negative views about Black folk are correct. Being afraid of difference is accepting that no one else is lovable and loved. Diversity education cannot happen if children do not learn to love themselves, their culture, their difference. Without a sincere appreciation of one's uniqueness, how will children learn to sincerely care about the difference in others?

Our experience is that when children do not have this appreciation of themselves during these young ages, the tendency is to reject or idolize the difference of others. When you are insecure within yourself, you might be pressured to emulate the behaviors and attitudes of others that are esteemed highly in our society. So the acceptance of Black inferiority in little ways may be inadvertently teaching Black children to fear presumed White superiority, when the reality couldn't be further from the truth.

When Black Children Ponder Being White

For decades psychologists have been studying why some (not all) Black youth choose White dolls over Black dolls when given the opportunity. Recent research has found that children have chosen these dolls because they have learned that the world appreciates Whiteness. As they get older, most youth lose the desire for this type of showy Whiteness. It does not mean that they hate their Blackness; it means they want all of the appreciation that the world ascribes to Whiteness or White people or White things. From the child's perspective, he or she may think to himself or herself, "I want to be White." Instead what it means for most children is "I want the freedom that all White people seem to have."

My sister called me to tell me once that she was worried about her four-year-old daughter, Kara, and that maybe she was not giving her enough experiences around other Black children. She was worried that she hadn't raised her right because Kara was making statements about the skin color of her parents. My sister is light brown skinned, and her husband is medium brown skinned. Esther said once that "Mommy, you're White, and Daddy and I are Black!" My sister was worried that somehow Kara didn't know as much about racial dynamics as she should have. I told her that her daughter was smart because she was learning and commenting on distinctions and colors. To be funny I told her that she shouldn't worry because Kara won't understand the psychology of institutional racism and/or the effects of global warming on Black people for at least two more years.

࿔

As kids get older, their awareness of American society's value of "Whiteness" increases. So a number of dilemmas may arise, such as the relative value placed on the image of Whiteness. Black children at this age who ponder wanting to be White do so not because they want to change their biological racial substance. They want the freedom to choose, they want the greater margin of error, and they want what every child wants—fun. And White people and White children on television look like they are having fun.

But fun can be reframed. When Howard Stevenson's son, Bryan, once asked about why he couldn't get certain toys or watch certain shows or be like certain people, Howard would grab him and start to hug or tickle him and ask, "Can a toy do this?" And Bryan would giggle a little, then start to object, and Howard would tickle some more and ask, "Can a toy do this?" Bryan would giggle even more. Then, after several bouts of this back and forth, Bryan would stop asking, and often it would end up in rough-and-tumble playtime.

Bryan always wanted to have fun. But the best fun was with loving, caring family members. And nothing can take the place of that. Bryan would forget the loss of the toy long enough to be distracted by other things. But basically, these and other strategies are not just meant to distract but to send a psychological message: no material image or thing is going to give you the same satisfaction as our relationship or an appreciation of yourself as a person. This is a hard lesson to learn, but it is a lifelong process. The challenge of watching Whites have "fun" is to help our children see that they can have fun that is more real, more natural, and available.

Protection for four- to eleven-year-olds involves the hypervigilance of parents to stay abreast of how society's racial intolerance will affect our children. But it also involves being there when our children are involved in plays, concerts, fairs, teacher meetings, and so on. Watching our children show off their talents is so important to their healthy psychological development. Protecting our children will also involve the basics of shelter, but we must not forget the psychological protection they will need to defend against the "blues" that come from being Black in a White man's world.

Who's Watchin' Over Whom? When Children See the Obvious

Parents aren't the only ones who are watchin' over. Children watch their parents too. They watch parents more than parents know or even want to know. Children between four and eleven years old begin to see the things that parents mean but don't say.

Unfortunately, adults learn to swallow their feelings, couch what they say, repress their anger, pretend to be nice, instigate irrelevant conflicts, or avoid direct conflicts. At this age children have not yet learned how to ignore and be quiet about the obvious. That's something they pick up later, as they get closer to their teen years. What is the obvious? Well, to a child, the obvious could be as simple as a situation where the mother and father are yelling at each other with intense angry looks on their faces. The child walks into the room, and both parents immediately stop what they are doing and simultaneously say, "Hey, baby, how are you doing?" Then the conversation goes something like this:

CHILD: Were you and Daddy fighting?
PARENTS: *(Together)* Oh, no, no.
MOTHER: We were just talking.

This and a hundred other examples represent how children sometimes go a little nuts trying to figure their parents out. But one issue is clear: children often learn that parents don't always mean what they say. Ironically, this is the time that children read the family dynamics (functional and dysfunctional) accurately, even if they don't understand all the details. This is also a reason why some children act out or get in trouble—because they are responding to the obvious troublesome messages that families send to their children without knowing it.

Sometimes when parents fight or refuse to resolve their marital disputes, the house is filled with enormous tension, which children pick up on and internalize. One way they handle the tension is to swallow all their feelings. Another way is to get into trouble to distract the family from the tension by drawing attention (albeit negative) to the child's behavior. A good family therapist or counselor can see right through this and can alert the family to how the child is crying for help to deal with the larger familial tension between parents.

Now, all families do functional and dysfunctional things. It's normal, so don't get scared. Because children listen to how family members talk to each other daily and because they are developmentally learning how to be human, they are more prepared to make sense of the meanings being communicated. So they pick up on the obvious. Sometimes the obvious (like marital or relationship dissatisfaction) that parents refuse to see makes children feel less safe. And we know what happens to kids when they don't feel safe—they react and act out and get spoiled. What do you do when your child doesn't feel safe? Pick up on the obvious. Take care of your marital or relationship business. Ask for help and model for your child how to handle marital or relationship tension, for example.

∽

The egg teaches the hen how to hatch.

∽

GETTIN' WITH: TEACHING REFLECTION AND SAFETY BY INSPIRING FREEDOM AND SETTING LIMITS

I got spanked as a kid, and I turned out okay. What's wrong with it? Nothing. As long as you don't go overboard, it's all right, right? That's what's wrong with kids today. They don't know how to listen, and they have no respect for their parents. Right?

∽

Gettin' With, or correction, for children age four to eleven is about teaching them the meaning of limits and teaching them to reflect on those limits. From this experience children can feel safer about what will happen to them. Unfortunately, without a combination of limits and reflection, children are left to make complex decisions on their own or follow the letter of the law but not the spirit of the law. Their anxiety will increase because of this and may influence their behavior.

Superficial Obedience

Without structure children will be left to make decisions that are too hard for them. At four, children need to know what is expected of them, and parents have to set clear limits and consequences for them to follow. So when children are disobedient, they need to know that parents will follow through with consequences, on a consistent basis.

Seeing the obvious family dynamics that parents avoid can lead to less security for the child. Parents often respond to child behavior that is excessive by becoming more rigid in their discipline strategies.

With too much structure or rigidity, parents are likely to create a superficially obedient child. This child is like the Stepford wives in that movie where all the women are robots and are meant to be seen and not heard or who don't have anything meaningful to say. They are often nonreflective and follow orders but not the meaning of the orders. They know the difference between right and wrong but not always why.

Why Many Parents Use Physical Punishment

1. False sense of competence in the moment (internal and external, what others may see and what you may feel)
2. Visceral or physical relief (for example, cessation of noise)
3. Outward respect or compliance in the moment
4. Anger related to unresolved childhood pain

Some kids who are superficially obedient know how to appease parents' fears. They may be able to make parents fear less by being obedient immediately to keep parents from investigating further. Parents who look forward to getting their fears reduced or who do not stay on top of their children's behavior will sometimes be shocked to find their eight- to eleven-year-olds involved in behaviors they were unaware of.

Is Fear Better Than Respect?

For many Black parents that we grew up with, there was a common phrase that folks used to say: "The problem with that child is that somebody needs to put the fear of God into him!" Some of us knew this to be a spanking, and others of us believed this to be more church time; sometimes it meant both.

We believe that the "fear of God" is more about the fear of Daddy or Mommy than God. Basically, we think the biblical sense of the fear of God is misunderstood. Most people are assuming that putting the fear of God into a child is to place inside of her the fear of some final judgment or punishment that she will no longer be able to get away from. To some, fear of God is fear of punishment for doing wrong.

If we look at the biblical interpretation of the fear of God, we find that sometimes it is definitely interpreted as dread or fear—but occurring when fear is used without God. When fear is attached to God in the Old and New Testament, it is often meant in the Greek and Hebrew versions to be attached to love, reverence, and awe. It is more about the fear of displeasing God, of not giving God reverence and honor, than about fear that God will punish. This fear is present whether one does wrong or not. It is an awesome thing to be able to realize that one's existence in the world is made possible by a Creator who loves us in spite of our limitations. The thinking behind this interpretation is that displeasing God is much more of a negative outcome than any punishment one could receive would be.

Why is fear attached to love and reverence? Because nothing could bring one more of a sense of meaninglessness than to disappoint the Creator, who has provided ultimate unconditional love. So when parents are saying to "put the fear of God" in the child, they could really be meaning to teach children how awesome it is to be loved by a Creator who is larger than our faults and our talents—and that this Creator is worthy of the ultimate respect.

So respect is better than fear, if what we mean by "fear" is punishment. Why? Because children are more likely to understand the meaning of correction if they respect and trust their parents than if they are afraid of their parents' wrath. Children who fear their parents are more likely to be obedient in their presence but not in their

absence. If children trust and respect parents, they are more likely
to hear and remember the meaning of the words parents say, not just
the words themselves. We believe intense fear may influence behavior, but it may also reduce reflection on what the behavior means.

Children are obeying out of fear if they

1. Shrink in fear when you raise your voice

2. Do what you say when you are around but not when
   you aren't

3. Understand the words you say but not the reason
   behind them

4. Are not sure what to do in situations where they have
   to make their own decisions about right and wrong

When children obey out of fear, they may

1. Experience temporary fear and seek to avoid it at all
   costs

2. Become desensitized to humiliation and fear

3. Look for ways to sneak around when parents are not
   there

4. Lie as a way to save face in public for themselves
   and their parents

When Parents Use Force, Is It Bad?

The use of physical discipline is not only an issue in the Black community. We are often forced by media portrayals of Black family life
to believe that physical violence is the sole means of discipline used
by African Americans. We are also led to believe that in all cases
physical discipline is a major cause of later aggression in teenagers.
The reality is that all families, from a variety of ethnic and racial backgrounds, engage in physical discipline.

Even more important, recent studies have shown that when African American and European American parents are compared, the use of physical discipline has different effects on their children. For European American parents there is a link between physical discipline and later child aggression. In one study the link did not exist for Black youth whose parents used physical discipline. But there remains more research to be accomplished on this matter.

If we hurl a stone into a market, it is usually our own kin whom it hits in the eye.

This finding supports research by Diane Baumrind (1972) of almost thirty years ago. In her work she found that, in general, parents use one of three styles of parenting: authoritarian, authoritative, or permissive. Authoritarian parenting is defined as high in control and low in nurturance, permissive parenting is high in nurturance but low in control, and authoritative parenting is moderate in both nurturance and control.

Of these three strategies, authoritative was perceived as the best parenting style, whereas authoritarian was associated with harsh discipline and resulted in more pathology among the children of White families. Permissive parenting led to children who were more disruptive and out of control. Interestingly enough, these findings did not hold for Black parents, who were found to be high in authoritarianism. Baumrind found that children of Black parents who used authoritarian parenting styles did not have pathological outcomes but in fact showed competent, assertive, and prosocial behavior, especially girls. What makes sense is that cultural style and strategies are in the mix of tough directive discipline strategies by many African American parents such that the "toughness" is not separated from the "nurturance."

This is how we believe the behaviors of Black parents are often misinterpreted by Whites who don't understand or pick up on the cultural messages that are communicated through some parenting strategies. The loudness of voice and sternness of look in some communities is viewed as authoritarian, narrowly defined, but to many Black families there is love in those looks and caring in that loudness. These are intimate cultural differences within and between racial groups in our society, and they are easily missed. Sometimes force means not oppression but clarity of focus.

∾

Scandal is like an egg: when it is hatched,
it has wings.

∾

"Because I Said So": To Spank or Not to Spank

The reality is that most parents borrow from their parents' effective *and* ineffective strategies. The discipline that we've seen and experienced as children becomes our training ground, even though we hate to admit it. Spanking has the interesting effect of leading us to find excuses for our parents and merging the bad experiences with the good.

When we conduct parenting workshops, we are amazed at how many parents are willing to defend their family's physical discipline by saying, "I got spanked, and I turned out all right!" We do not disagree with these folks but ask a few questions like, "Did the spanking always stop you from engaging in the negative behavior?" or "Did it always work?" and "Do you ever feel like your parents went too far?" These questions open up a Pandora's box of emotions, which often allows us to present the possibility that spanking is not always helpful and to propose what parents can do about those times.

Parents go through struggles when they use or contemplate using physical discipline. We encourage readers to reflect seriously and to consider the possibility that the discipline they experienced as children was not as "good" as it was cracked up to be. We encourage parents to realize that all individuals want to romanticize their childhood.

It can certainly be painful to reflect on those experiences that were hurtful or humiliating.

Context is very important in making sense of physical discipline, however. It matters whether or not parents are helpless when they are applying discipline. It matters whether they are communicating protection, affection, and responsibility in their discipline strategies. Physical discipline is less necessary if a child is part of a larger network of relationships. We want parents to gain a keen understanding of how children teach us a lot about ourselves as we try to discipline them.

Discipline works best when children trust their parents. To separate discipline from trust is like having a house with no heat in the wintertime. Even though you have a roof over your head, you may still freeze to death. Parents who instill fear rather than trust will often build a house made of mortar but fail to heat the people in it. And then we wonder why our children are cold. Some parents are the "Just be glad you have a roof over your head" parent, and they are absolutely right about their children being protected from the outside. But they are not as protected on the inside. In this book we want to go further. We want parents to make the connection between their children's verbal and nonverbal behaviors with the prescription that they listen to what their children are saying and not saying. This is discipline that children can trust and use to keep themselves warm inside and outside of the house.

Children do not easily separate caring and correction. Until we understand the key ingredients to parenting, we will struggle to understand why our children are sometimes confused about what we mean. If we use physical force, we are sometimes adding more confusion to an already confusing situation. We know that changing one's use of physical discipline is hard. Why?

Why Changing One's Use of Physical Discipline Is So Hard

One reason is because it is like losing weight—it requires a change in lifestyle. It is more complicated than learning alternative discipline strategies. An example is when a parent is too stressed with life issues. Another example is when a parent or set of parents cannot restructure their lives in a way that will allow them to supervise the child when disciplined. Still another example is when parents are not in a position to apply a consistent set of rules. All of these examples make physical punishment a more likely option.

Things That Can Make It Hard to Change One's Use of Physical Discipline

1. One might be too stressed to stop and think about it.

2. Spanking can sometimes restore order in the moment.

3. Many parents who live in the moment will find that quick fixes tend to fit in nicely.

4. Parents are parenting the best they can under difficult circumstances.

5. It's what our parents did.

Second, for many stressed and overworked parents, physical punishment is a decisive, immediate response that works in the moment. It can have long-term consequences, but you don't always think of this if other issues preoccupy your mind. Often, to apply a quick strategy and see immediate results can make many parents feel confident. Unfortunately, we believe it is a false sense of confidence that doesn't last very long. And as we said earlier, it might also impress other families who we feel are on our back about how to manage our children. Demonstrating through an immediate action that we are in control can address the other cultural fear that we may be lousy parents raising out-of-control Black kids. Our challenge to this view is that the tail is wagging the dog. The fear of what others will think—not affection and protection and our knowledge of our children—is driving our limit setting with our children.

Third, a spanking sometimes restores order, peace, and quiet in the moment. If you live your life in the moment, spanking sort of fits. Why would parenting practices differ from how we shop, prepare meals, wash clothes, and so on? But there is something to be said for stopping the *noise!*

Another reality we have to consider that makes changing one's discipline strategy so difficult is that folks are parenting the best they can under difficult circumstances. Our only challenge to this view is that this doesn't mean that it's the best that parents can do. Black parents did the best they could under slavery, but that doesn't mean that slavery is an appropriate environment for raising healthy Black children. But all of these reasons make it hard to change.

∝

What goes around comes around.

∝

If you feel that you are busy and overstressed, need peace and quiet, and are doing the best you can, it may be very hard to find a reason to change the use of spanking. But the biggest reason may be that it's what our parents did to us. Our suggestion is to remember the old proverb "What goes around comes around." If you make time now to use different strategies, you will find the results coming out when your child needs to be patient with himself or herself—when he or she is your age. If you are using the strategies that you experienced in your childhood, then what went around has already come around once. Take a look at it.

When Not to Use Physical Discipline

As you can tell, even when we find that parents use physical discipline and find it effective, we don't recommend it. We believe the long-term emotional consequences come back to haunt children and parents alike. But we do recognize that folks don't stop using spanking simply because policemen, judges, social workers, psychologists, counselors, or family tell them to stop. There have to be other ways to understand why parents feel the need to use physical discipline than simplistic strategies of "just say no," which do not work.

So that's why we want this book to appeal to parents who may use physical punishment with their children. Here are a few of our recommendations for parents who use spanking.

We don't recommend physical punishment, but for those of you who use it, we recommend that you don't use it

1. When you are under stress

2. When you are angry and in a rage

3. To humiliate or embarrass your child

4. When you have been drinking alcohol

5. To demonstrate your power and control to other adults

6. To show people how good a parent you are to have controlled kids

7. When you observe it does not work

8. When you see that your child is more likely to fear than respect you

9. When you observe that your child is unable or less able to share his voice or opinion out of fear

10. When you see your child using force to resolve issues and to get his way

11. When you hear your child say to a friend or to toys the very same words you say when you are angry or when you are punishing them

12. When your child only responds to being spanked

13. When you haven't fully received emotional help to

manage your own childhood traumas related to physical punishment

14. When your child has nightmares related to the discipline

Terry is a twenty-nine-year-old father of two children, Darren, age ten, and Sarae, age seven. He has used spanking as a way to discipline his children, but he is feeling that it's not working like it used to. In fact, it hasn't worked very well for a while. He realized that it gave him a false sense of security. It brought peace and quiet because everybody was afraid of his anger. But that peace was short-lived because he was tormented about whether he was doing the right thing. He attended some workshops on parenting in his church, and he has begun to feel a sense of sadness about the spankings because he remembers how his children look at him afterward. Usually he avoids thinking about these images. He always thought that spanking did him some good, but recently when he was asked if his own father's discipline helped him, he had to admit that sometimes he got the message and sometimes he just got angry and found new ways to rebel. Terry realized he didn't want his children going behind his back to prove to him that they don't like to be disciplined so harshly. He decided that he wanted to be a different father than what he experienced. He wanted to be a father who talked to his children and whose children talked to him. He decided to ask for help, and what he found out was that he was worried that he had to be tough on his children because the world would be tough on them because of the color of their skin. He was worried that they, as Black children, would have to deal with hardships that he could not always be there to help them through, and so by instilling a sense of toughness, it would be like carrying a piece of their father with them as they survived tough times. But he realized that this was a difficult lesson to learn through spanking and that there were other ways to address the fear of future racial and gender oppression than "hitting them to make them obey."

⁂

Now, please don't think we are suggesting that you shouldn't discipline your child. An undisciplined child within an African psychology framework is an unaware child. An unaware child is one who does not understand where he is when he misbehaves or how the world around him has barriers, limits, *and* opportunities.

Teaching the Egg to Hatch

When we use the African proverb "The egg teaches the hen how to hatch," we are saying that the child (either the child in us who has been long forgotten or our children) will teach us how to be better people, better humans—if only we listen. Listen to the child in you who got spanked and ask tougher questions. Don't just accept that the spankings you got were absolutely the right thing. They may have taught you a lot, but critiquing them will not erase the lessons you learned.

The both-and still applies to our childhood spankings. They may have taught us life lessons, but they may have left some scars of anger and resentment as well. Now, there is a thought! Is it possible that physical discipline leaves both positive and negative memories? All we are asking you to do is not deny, avoid, or put away the negative memories because they too are a part of your child, your life, you.

Frequently Asked Questions

- How did I handle tough love when it was given to me in my childhood?

- How can I be more prepared when I talk to my child about his behavior?

- Why is it so hard for me to say what I want to say to my child when it is time to correct her?

The results of a discipline strategy that integrates developmentally and culturally appropriate affection, protection, and correction are multiple and contagious. It is not far out of our reach to believe that children can learn a lot from alternative discipline strategies. Withholding enjoyable social activities is a key strategy. Some folks call this "time-out." Keeping a child from the social life he or she is developmentally ready for and desires to be part of can help the child rethink negative behavior. Time-out can be culturally relevant and developmentally appropriate. It can help children hear what you are meaning, not just what you are saying.

We don't recommend a lot of lecturing for children between the ages of four and eleven when they misbehave. The primary reason is that their attention span is short by nature. So we have a few guidelines about how to talk to your child when they are misbehaving.

Six Steps to Giving Your Child Tough Love Through Verbal Correction

1. *Think* about what you are going to say before you say it.

2. *Keep it short*—it should last no longer than thirty seconds.

3. *Practice* what you are going to say before you say it.

4. *Think* of the many ways your child will respond before you say it.

5. *Think* of the many ways you could respond to your child before you say it.

6. *Say it.*

A wise person speaks carefully and with truth, for every word that passes between one's teeth is meant for something.

Molefi Kete Asanti

The Look, the Grunt, and the Wagging Head: Nonverbal Discipline

My father had a look that would drop you to your knees in a hot minute. And you knew that you had done something wrong and that there was no need to argue because behind that look was the force of nature and power of the universe. Resistance is futile! Sometimes you didn't even have to see him looking at you, but you knew. You knew that he was giving you that look and punishment was imminent. The hairs on the back of my neck would stand to attention like privates at an admiral's ball, and your eyes looked heavenward praying ever so gently, "Lord, please, whatever it is, could you come down now and keep my daddy from whuppin' my butt!" And then I remembered what people in the church used to say— "Obedience is better than sacrifice"—and I just needed to stop doing whatever wrong thing I was doing, and the look would vanish as quickly as it came.

⁂

Nonverbal communication has played as significant a role as verbal communication in the lives of African Americans. For centuries African Americans have had to keep quiet out of fear of retribution. Today the fear of how one is perceived in public leads to more silent resistance and affirmation than open verbal resistance or affirmation, especially in predominantly White environments. Over time and as part of the culture, African Americans have become proficient in body language and interpretation of nonverbal communication. It's not just what you say, it's how you say it. And it doesn't matter whether you say it with your voice or your body, you are still speaking loudly.

When kids are between the ages of four and eleven, nonverbal discipline can go a long way to helping children save face socially. We encourage parents to continue to use these strategies as well as to learn the cultural meaning of these behaviors. To maximize the power of these techniques, we think it is important to examine key nonverbal behaviors like "the Look." The Look is a strategy that parents have used to train their children to be quiet in public places. The Look has many beneficial components. By applying the Look, parents can refrain from using verbal corrections when being loud would disrupt the public event, bring public humiliation, or lead to walking into stereotypes. It is also respectful of the child, who may be among his or her peers while engaging in the particular disturbance.

Howard Stevenson discusses how interpreting nonverbal behavior helped him with his son's mischief:

My son at five would do something he had no business doing, like taking a small toy to school to show to his friends. The problem was that he would give away that he did something wrong by the look on his face. It was a look that most kids give when they are hiding something. I would say, "Boy, what did you do?" And he would say, "How did you know?" And I would say back to him, "Don't you know that fathers can see everything you do? Remember that." This lasted for about three years before he caught on, but they were three good years.

⟳

Other nonverbal behaviors include stylistic intonations of voice and grunts that culturally communicate to children whole lessons on obedience, morality, and altruism. We have observed a host of nonverbal behaviors of children that similarly communicate whole treatises on resistance or revolutionary protest. Culturally, for example, rolling one's eyes to a parent is a serious statement about disrespect. Parents can do well to "call" these behaviors "on the carpet," if for no other reason than to let the child know that parents are attentive to all of their communications, even the subtle ones. Other examples include hands on the hips, finger wagging, staring one down, and biting one's tongue. Nonverbal communication represents a history of learned behaviors that protect parent and child alike in social arenas where cultural, parental, and social self-respect and competence are at stake. Parents can understand themselves and children better if they respect each other's nonverbal messages while paying close attention to them.

What Comes Around When We Use Affection, Protection, and Correction

It is toughest to love with discipline when parents are isolated and unsupported. We believe that when discipline is most effective, it happens within a community of extended family members and has several beneficial results for young Black children.

The Results of Effective Discipline for Young Black Children

1. Self-awareness and reflection
2. Community appreciation
3. Spiritual growth

It is our belief that children who are aware, who appreciate their community and the people in it, and can grow spiritually are children who will eventually contribute to the world in meaningful ways. A child who is self-aware is one who has strengths that will be called upon in the most difficult moments of his or her life. A child who is self-aware is one who usually trusts his parents to discipline him with affection, protection, and correction.

Children who are self-aware will

1. Be less frightened when other children assert their special talents
2. Not panic as much when they feel helpless inside
3. Be excited to show their talents when they are around others

4. Play with others in cooperative rather than competitive ways

5. Be more interested in keeping friends than dominating others

To have to be so hypervigilant about the world's racism is one way parenting Black children is different from parenting other children. This hypervigilance is like a big weight on one's shoulders daily, and many parents would rather not have to consider this burden at all. Although most definitions of racism involve something systemic and permanent, parents who deny the reality of racism as it applies to their and their children's lives may be unprepared to help their children manage the social world. If what goes around comes around, what do you want to come around for your child a year from now? Five years? Ten years? Twenty years? Think about it—because your children already have.

4

When Black Children Grow Wings, the World Gets Scared

Discipline and Preteens

Everybody needs a posse every now and then.

Gary and Sheila are two African American parents in their mid-thirties who are beginning to see the importance of teaching their son, Ahmad, about racism. But they don't know how. Ahmad is eleven, and his experiences in school are changing. Ahmad is growing bigger and faster than ever before, and he is looking more mature. He has always been a good student and cooperative with teachers, and he has both White and Black friends. At first, everyone loved Ahmad; he was one of the most likable boys in his class. His White and Black classmates invited him over to their homes for birthday parties and playtime. But Gary and Sheila have noticed that teachers have begun to raise issues about Ahmad's anger. They say he is resistant and argumentative with the teachers. They say he is sometimes aggressive with other kids. Ahmad has come home crying over racial names he has been called by Whites in the school who do not know him. They also notice that he isn't invited to play with his White friends as much. Sheila has noticed that Ahmad is starting to talk back to her more than ever.

༒

A s children become teenagers, boys become men, and girls become women, the world takes a dramatic wrong left turn. For many Black families and youth, it turns left, then backward. Or so it seems. One of the most challenging realities of being Black and near puberty is that not only do Black preteens feel like their bodies and the world change right before their eyes, but the world *does* change. It responds differently to Black youth than to other youth in America.

WHEN CHILDREN GROW WINGS: THE BEGINNING OF REBELLION OR THE END OF CHILDHOOD?

Preadolescence is hard for all preteens, but when you add the burden of racism, preadolescence is more than a developmental period. It's more than an adventure. It can be hell. For some Black youth the threat or pain of racism is unknown, not felt, not identified. Unfortunately, like low-frequency static, racism mutters in the background, sometimes increasing in volume for a moment to maintain status quo then disappearing again to a hum. Many Black youth can't always see or hear the hum because they may have not been trained to hear it.

The magic and madness of adolescence is that teens know just enough to know that experience is the best teacher, yet they don't have enough experience to know that listening, watching, and waiting are the most reliable experiences. The magic and madness of parenting adolescents is that parents remember just enough of adolescence to realize how serious it can be, but they forget too much of it to be empathetic. Parenting adolescents is more than a lifelong acquaintance with helplessness; it is a life's worth of helplessness squeezed into six years (between twelve and eighteen years old).

For many Black parents resistance from children is hard to tolerate. Why? Well, many of the racial struggles we face in society are considered to be enough heartache. The last thing we want to deal with when we come home from a disrespectful society is to have to put up with a disrespectful child. The phrase "I brought you into this world, and I can take you out" was made nationally famous by Bill

Cosby when he spoke these words to Theo as Theo decided he wanted to defy his parents and refuse to go to school. This *Bill Cosby Show* episode hit home for many Black parents across social classes. But this phrase has been one of many common phrases among Black parents who have tired of normal developmental resistance from budding preadolescents. So there are a host of phrases that Black parents say that seem to reflect the frustration of this period.

Phrases Frustrated Black Parents Say to Preteens

1. "Boy, I brought you into this world, and I can take you out."
2. "I don't care how old you get, remember you are never too old to get [chastised]."
3. "You're getting too grown for your age. If you think you can take care of yourself, move out."
4. "Your body is outgrowing your mind, girl."
5. "Have you lost your mind!"
6. "If you want to live in my house, you gotta live by my rules."
7. "You know better than that."
8. "Boy, you are way too old to be doing stuff like that!"
9. "Because I said so!"
10. "How dare you . . ."

Preadolescents must test the limits of their parents as a rite of passage. Anything less might be unthinkable. So how does a preteen try and demonstrate to the world that she is more than a dependent, submissive, untalented, broke, sit-around-the-house, do-everything-your-parents-tell-you-to-do child? *Resistance* is how.

No wonder this period is often considered the most difficult for parents and teachers because children are growing in more ways than one. Parents are expecting more independence from preteens who are still needing dependence yet beginning to demand less monitoring. So how do African American parents manage the challenges of protection, affection, and correction for preteens? Slowly, very slowly. Let's start with affection.

STICKIN' TO: HUGGING FROM A DISTANCE

It is a challenge to be physically affectionate toward a resistant, constantly disagreeable, smart-mouthed, moody, disrespectful preteen. The challenge is to be able to manage your emotions while at the same time understanding her. It seemed like just yesterday she would crawl up into your arms, and now you have to literally drag her just to give you some affection. This pull and tug can shake the foundation of even the most stable parent.

If we are boastful parents (and many of us are), we may be caught in the trap of having told other people, families, and friends just how well we know our children—only to find out they are becoming someone different right before our very eyes. It's like the movie *The Exorcist,* where one minute your child is sick and cuddly, wanting affection and staying home from school, and the next minute he's spewing bile at you. Or every time you walk into his room, it's so cold from the hostility and the looks you get, you swear you are in an icebox. Well, have no fear—this is exactly what most parents are normally afraid of when it comes to parenting preteens. Sometimes the chill comes from violating the child's personal space (that is, their room), and other times there's no explanation for the chilly response.

Humorous Ways to Know Your Child Is Becoming a Preteen

1. You swear he's possessed by the devil.

2. You swear the devil has at least visited her bedroom.

3. Every time you watch the evening news and see Black teens in handcuffs, all you can see is your son ending up in jail.

4. You read an article titled "What's Wrong with Parents Today" and wonder who your child has been talking to.

5. You read an article on the top ten emotional disorders affecting children and swear they're talking about your child.

6. You notice that you are swearing more now than you ever have in your entire life.

7. The concept of justifiable homicide starts to make more and more sense.

So, as we have said from the beginning of this book, don't let your fears get the best of you. But there is one particular cycle you may want to be aware of: the cycle of emotional rejection.

The Cycle of Emotional Rejection

In our conversations with Black parents over the last ten years, we have found that many frustrations at nurturing preteens come from the head-to-head battles. These battles are new, and parents are beginning to see them for the first time. Preteens have more facility of speech and make more logical arguments that make sense. Sometimes they argue a point better than parents because they have more time to think about it. Parents are often taken aback by the quality of the resistance. The shock at being disputed or disrespected is so overwhelming for many African American parents. Partly it's because the child is moving away from you in a new way. But to be "checkmated" by a twelve-year-old whom you remember just yesterday holding in your arms is too much to take. And that can lead to the famous "Child, you better #$@#%^ before I #$@#%^!"

proclamation. Parents under these circumstances pull the "because I said so" card.

We think these battles are places where all parents must communicate caring and accountability. They must appreciate their children's growing developmental abilities to reason and stand up for themselves while at the same time helping them understand the limits to their newfound social skills. The mistake many parents make is to squelch these wonderful expressions of self-knowledge. Black parents who are also burdened by the racial disrespect of the world may find these childish adultlike behaviors to be much of the same thing and become livid: "You think I'm going to let any child of mine talk like that to me? I don't think so!"

But these social skills of standing up for oneself and arguing a point are very important to Black youth's ability to survive and self-actualize in the competitive world of adults and peers. Preteens are beginning to learn how to reason and trust themselves so that life obstacles are not overwhelming. Standing up for themselves allows them to not shrink from difficulty and to assert their God-given and parent-taught skills of self-reliance. Your children will need this assertiveness to reject the racial hostilities of the employers, car dealers, and institutional authorities they will run into who expect them to be ignorant. Don't squelch this. Channel it. You helped to create it!

When this clash occurs, affection, protection, and correction can get distorted. Figure 4.1 depicts the way such a cycle can end up in the loss of affection and protection across time when parents don't allow for the developmental strivings of their children.

The battle between parents and preteens can create in children a sense of injustice that sometimes gets compared to the social injustices of Black-on-Black violence, taxation without representation, and global warming. This can trigger more resistance in the child, which in turn leads to parents feeling betrayed (especially those who are unprepared for these developmental strivings). "How dare you . . ." is often the beginning of a statement that reflects a certain level of betrayal. Of all of the emotions that a parent can feel, betrayal may be a new one and may throw the parent off guard.

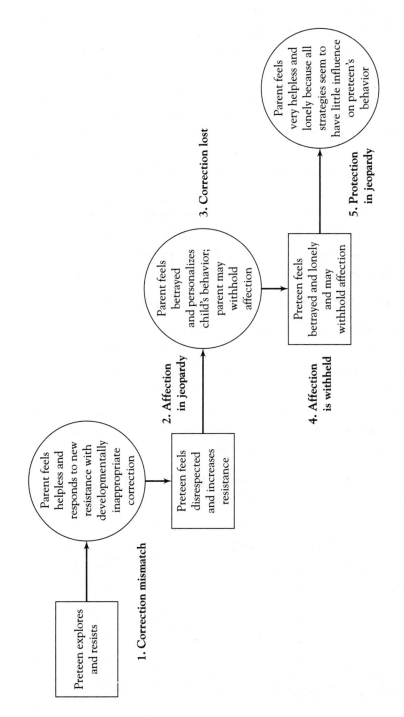

Figure 4.1. How Affection, Protection, and Correction Get Lost When You Are Parenting Preadolescents.

Black parents who feel they have sacrificed life, limb, future, past, and culture to raise their child may feel betrayed not only as a parent but as a Black parent who has unique obligations to fulfill. One of those obligations is raising a respectful Black child, and during the head-to-head battles the vision of fulfilling this obligation starts to dim. So some parents may unconsciously withdraw their affection as a way to protect themselves, and feelings of betrayal always lead to self-protection, less giving of affection, and sometimes more punishment. Over time both parent and child can feel emotionally isolated and abandoned.

Often preteens experience the old ways of punishment as childish and harsh given their newfound social skills, body changes, and peer relationships. So they often fight back in little ways when they are treated, corrected, nurtured, or protected in childish ways.

Single-Parent Struggles with Preteens

We have often witnessed how single parents can receive hostility and tribulations from preteens based on the preteens' submerged anger at the absent parent (if that parent is not meaningfully involved in the life of the child). Preteens often need a sounding board, and the single parent is often the only one available. These parents need extra support for these moments. Culturally, mothers have often had to bear the burden of these clashes.

Avoiding the Cycle of Rejection: Apologizing, Appreciating, and Negotiating

We hope understanding the cycle can help parents avoid it. First, once you recognize that your strategies are outdated or excessive, apologize. The sentiment of correction was on the right track, but the strategy might have been belittling.

Ways to Avoid the Cycle of Rejection

1. *Apologize* when you as a parent go too far in applying your correction strategies to obvious misbehavior.

> 2. *Appreciate* the preteen's developmental needs to explore the world.
>
> 3. *Negotiate* the consequences by involving the preteen in the application and explanation of the consequences of the misbehavior.

For example, let's say Ahmad came home a few hours late after being outside with friends. Gary and Sheila went looking for him, found him down the street with his friends, and scolded him in front of his friends. To correct him was the right thing to do. To spank him or to yell at him in front of his friends, however, may create that sense of humiliation and resentment that could trigger the cycle. Apologizing for the humiliation yet providing an appropriate consequence for the lateness is one way to avoid the cycle of rejection. Appreciating that the preteen has growing developmental needs to look and act "mature" can give him the sense that his parents are old and annoying but not ancient, tyrannical, and uncaring.

Here is an example of how Gary and Sheila, in the scenario just described, might apologize for the humiliation but provide an appropriate consequence:

GARY: Son, how many times have we told you how dangerous it is for you to stay out past a certain time?

SHEILA: We are getting tired of saying the same thing over and over again.

AHMAD: (*Fuming and looking down*) But see, there—

GARY: Don't "but" me. Because you disobeyed us, you will have to suffer the consequences.

SHEILA: Yes, but first we want to say we're sorry for embarrassing you in front of your friends.

AHMAD: (*Looking up with anger but slightly amazed his parents understood his anger*) Well, those kids were laughing at me! Now I won't be able to hang out with them anymore. How am I going to face them? They're going to talk about me like—(*sighing with frustration and dejection, shoulders slumping, as if simultaneously giving up a battle and letting off steam*)

GARY: If you had come in when we told you, that would not have happened. But it still isn't right to embarrass you. I lost my head. I was so mad that you disobeyed me, I started yelling before I realized what I was saying.

SHEILA: Yes, me too.

(*Ahmad looks around, wondering if this joint apology is for real, and is perplexed that this shift in his parents from punishment to apology actually takes some of the sting out of his anger. He kind of stares quizzically into space, speechless.*)

In addition, Gary and Sheila should appreciate Ahmad's developmental need to "hang out" with the boys. The dialogue should now focus on understanding the experience of preteenhood, which can further reduce the hostility in Ahmad's soul about being mistreated:

GARY: Your mother and I also want you to know that we know it's hard being your age. Kids your age love to hang out. I used to do the same thing. Sometimes it was hard for me to come inside when your grandparents would call me in.

SHEILA: I'm not going to tell you what my mother or father would do if I didn't come in on time. Even if I knew I would get in trouble, I would want to stay with my girlfriends. But I learned not to. And that's what you have to do.

AHMAD: You stayed out late too, Mom?

SHEILA: Ahmad, of course, but not for long. My parents would worry like crazy that something would happen.

GARY: And that's where we are right now. Worried that something could happen with you hanging out past a certain time.

Finally, negotiating affection can give the preteen more freedom in the decision making in your relationship. Giving preteens more decision-making power in your relationship with them can relieve some of the battles yet still make your word the final word in the matter. Here is how Gary and Sheila might end their dialogue with Ahmad:

GARY: So we understand why you want to stay out with your friends. We're not saying you can't hang out with them.

SHEILA: Do you understand that?

AHMAD: Yes.

GARY: But you *have* to come in when we tell you.

SHEILA: Do you understand that?

AHMAD: Yes.

SHEILA: Do you also understand that we have to give you a consequence because you disobeyed?

AHMAD: Yes, but please don't take away my going outside. Please.

GARY AND SHEILA: Well, it's either that or no television and PlayStation for three days.

AHMAD: PlayStation.

GARY AND SHEILA: Do you also realize that if you disobey again, you will lose your "hangout time" immediately?

AHMAD: (*Feeling relieved but stung by the fact that he will have to do something different with his room time*) Do y'all promise not to embarrass me anymore in front of my friends?

GARY AND SHEILA: Yes, but we will come and get you if you disobey. Your best choice is to come in on time, little man. Do you understand?

AHMAD: *(Reluctant but settled)* Yes.

Parents at this point can decide to shake on it or hug, then apply the consequence immediately. The key in this dialogue or one like it is that you stop the cycle of rejection that can escalate into adolescence on every matter, not just one. Also, kids have transacted with the discipline instead of just receiving the discipline. By apologizing for correction that is a bit overboard, appreciating the developmental needs of the preteen, and negotiating the consequences of the misbehavior, parents are inviting children into the discipline process. This increases the chances that your child will internalize the meaning of discipline, not just seek ways to fight against it because they don't understand it or find it unjust.

Hug Them Anyhow

Negotiating before you apply the consequences of misbehavior should always involve some type of affection. Why? Because it can connect caring with correction and make it easier for your child to accept the consequences. You can't always expect your preteen to accept the consequences graciously, nor should you wait until they agree before you apply the consequences. In fact, don't pick easy consequences. The child should "suffer the consequences." But negotiation allows for affection and correction to be consolidated, establishing an atmosphere in which communication is a major way to solve conflicts.

You may have to be creative, but never stop showing physical affection toward your preteen, whether you are correcting them or not. She needs to know that you still care in demonstrative ways because the "child" she is leaving developmentally is still alive, just invisible. So sometimes the hugs have to be private. We recommend that you make a pact with your child that you promise not to embarrass them in public if they promise to give you a hug regularly. The pact could also include that they need to be hugged as part of their growth as a human being, and you as the parent are the only one who can give your kind of affection.

And you might want to negotiate spontaneous expression of affection zones (SPAZ—as in when you "spaz out" on your child) and forget their needs for public maturity and coolness. These SPAZ moments come when your child has scored points in a game or they got an A or they have told you something to surprise you. It is imperative that parents negotiate SPAZ moments so that they won't be held accountable for uncontrollable affection should their child shock them with his behavior or should they be so excited at her success. You know yourself and know exactly under what conditions you are likely to spaz out. If you don't, get some help from friends, loved ones, or professionals and reread Chapter One of this book. Ask a girlfriend or a homie or a family member. Don't promise what you can't deliver, or else your child will go back on his agreement too— and the cycle of rejection could begin.

GETTIN' WITH: WHEN LAYING DOWN THE LAW GETS A LITTLE MURKY

Kids are growing up and getting harder, so your strategies of discipline have to grow up too. The good news is that you survived preadolescence yourself; the bad news is that the skills you used are outdated.

If you are still using physical punishment and your child is eleven, you've probably got a bigger problem that a whuppin' won't solve. This is really where parents learn the lesson that control is a fantasy. Now they can stay out late. They can defy you. They have mobility. They have hip-hop.

You know your discipline strategies are developmentally outdated when

1. You find your preteen frequently accusing you of "treating him like a child"

2. Your preteen reminds you of the stories you used to tell of your adolescence

3. You still think preteens will do things just because you told them to

4. You swear your preteen would "never do anything like that" behind your back

5. You think she is likely losing her mind

6. Taking away TV time doesn't have the same effect

7. Your preteen, as a statement of protest, begs you to take away the TV and the PlayStation and threatens a hunger strike to boot

8. You can no longer bluff, make idle threats, talk loud, or use strong parental gestures and expect your preteen to back down

9. You are overcome by an overwhelming sense of helplessness whenever you start to discipline your preteen (saying to yourself, "This will never work")

10. Your preteen starts to make logical arguments about why your strategies don't work, and you begin to agree

11. You think you can keep your preteen from hearing music that has bad language simply because you tell them "not to listen to that stuff"

12. You think hip-hop is a bunny rabbit

13. You think that when you say *"No!"* your preteen will think the conversation is over

> **14.** You think that your preteen has only one plan A for disobeying you and forget that she now knows how to think about plans B, C, D, and E

Outdated discipline strategies are a Black parent's nightmare and can only trigger the cycle of rejection between parents and children. When children feel rejected, they may resort to multiple ways to avoid the punishment or discipline of parents who are also feeling rejected. So in addition to warning parents to avoid the cycle of rejection and to update their parenting strategies, we want to help them keep from misinterpreting the situation when their children lie to them.

When Children Lie: Lying Is Not a Character Flaw

∽

Not to know is bad; not to want to know is worse.

∽

Frequently Asked Questions

- What should I do when I catch my child in a lie?

- What if my child catches me in a lie?

- I can't stand lying, but sometimes I go overboard. I don't want him to grow up to be a dishonest person. What can I say to my child so that lying does not become a habit?

Many of us struggle with the notion of "truth" throughout our lives. This struggle begins in childhood and preteenhood as we become aware that we have thoughts, experiences, and ideas that are independent of those of our parents. Preteens know that they don't like spinach but that their parents do. Preteens think parents think that rap music is a bad influence, whereas preteens simply like the way it sounds. It is at this point that the child is truly becoming a separate, autonomous being with thoughts, experiences, and ideas independent of (and often very different from) those of his parents. The parent's definition of "truth" is no longer applicable. This developmental stage requires that the child ask himself, "What is truth?" Is it whatever my mother says, is it what I see or experience myself, or is it whatever I say it is? Lying is the child's way of exploring the essence of truth by asking himself, "Is the truth something that I can manipulate?" and "Did I do it if no one saw me do it?" Although the experimentation with the truth starts earlier, preteens experiment with lying in more visible ways.

The Stages of Lying

1. The child realizes that the parent is neither omniscient nor omnipresent.
2. The child wants to avoid discipline or punishment.
3. The child experiences increasing independence from parents.
4. The child struggles with the process of exploring the meaning and relevance of truth.
5. The child experiments with lying.
6. The parent responds to the child's lie.
7. The child either (a) feels a sense of guilt and remorse and wants to avoid these feelings in the future or (b) finds that the lie has served his purpose and determines that lies are useful and perhaps even necessary.

Why Children Lie

Why does lying happen? As parents, we sometimes find it difficult to recall our own experience with "taking liberties with the truth."

Somehow we can never quite remember having struggled in this area, and if we do, our struggles seem to pale in comparison with our children's. To put it simply, children lie for three reasons: to avoid punishment, to test the bounds of truth, and to avoid shame for what they have or have not done. In the mind of the preteen, lying is sometimes unavoidable because the burden of shame, guilt, or punishment outweighs the lofty benefits of truth and honesty. Some children would rather their parents spank them than lecture them, because words can touch the soul and trigger shame and guilt in a person. Children do not have the adults' perspective that telling the truth outweighs the feelings of intense shame and guilt for doing something wrong. Preteens are just pondering this possibility but need to run some tests first.

Lying Is a Contradiction—So Apologize, Appreciate, and Negotiate

When kids catch their parents in a lie, it is important that parents take the time to explain and admit the mistake or they risk teaching children that lying is okay. Imagine a situation in which a parent is busy at home working, the phone rings, and the call is for the parent. The daughter, who is twelve, answers the phone but receives a silent signal from the parent that says, "Tell them I'm not home." This type of conversation might follow:

> DAUGHTER: When I said I didn't break your vase, you said that was a lie. But when you said you weren't home and you were, why isn't that a lie?

The parent's words and actions at this point are important. The parent should apologize if she has been caught in a lie. She shouldn't try to justify it, because if she does, she will pay for it later.

> PARENT: You're right. I am sorry. Lying under any circumstances is not right. I just have a lot of work to do. Still, that doesn't make it right.

Negotiating the consequence doesn't apply here, but the parent can negotiate how they both will handle this situation in the future.

PARENT: What I should have said to you was to tell the person on the phone that I was busy right now and would call them back later. I was right in the middle of some good work, and I needed some space and time to think without being interrupted. But I should have said that to you. My fault. Next time I'll do a better job, okay? Let's both not get in the habit of not telling the whole truth.

DAUGHTER: Okay.

Again, you are appreciating the preteen's growing developmental abilities to figure out social situations as well as accurately interpret your lessons. To reinforce this is only to teach her that her instincts are good. This can only add to her self-esteem. Finally, negotiate how you want the situation to go. This allows for the child to understand your underlying reasons for refusing the phone call. Often we have no logical reason for not telling the whole truth; it's just easier to avoid the call. But when our youth are involved, they are watching the whole story, not just the bylines.

The Problem Is Not Lying But the Commitment to It

The problems arise when preteens are good at lying and then begin to perfect their skills. When this happens, it can affect their character. Usually, it takes parents' falling asleep in the area of correction and protection for this to occur without being witnessed. Parents should help their children to understand that lying isn't necessary. Be concerned when your child is committed to a lie or doesn't see a lie as problematic as long as they are not getting caught. Children should have an appreciation of the consequences and meaning of lying as well as an appreciation of the benefits that come from a trusting relationship. But when a child lies, it does not necessarily mean that the child will become a criminal for life, even though parents fear this possibility every day. Remember that our society condones a certain level of lying that is not just acceptable but that produces success; so don't hesitate to point out these unfortunate contradictions.

What to Do

Try to figure out why a child lies, in order to apply the best consequence. The motivation behind the lie is crucial for a parent to know. Some kids lie out of fear of disappointing a parent, getting punished, or both. Some lie out of a desire to save face with friends by doing things they know parents wouldn't approve of. But these are different motivations. A liar is someone who makes lying a lifestyle, but someone who lies out of fear is making a mistake that deserves correction, protection, and affection, not just punishment. If children can experience the consequences of lying, they are less likely to continue it. For example, telling a lie that gets another child in trouble may seem harmless if the child who told the lie does not have to hear the feelings of anguish from the "victim." Having the victim share what happened as a result of the lie can stimulate remorse and empathy because of the situation the lie led to.

What to Do When Your Child Lies to You

1. Don't overreact or ignore it entirely. Make sure the discipline fits the crime.

2. Focus on behaviors you want her to do, not on what you want her to stop doing.

3. Remember the feelings you had when you once lied.

4. Show your child how their lying hurts other people's feelings and opportunities.

5. Don't make them feel like a liar because they told a lie.

6. Understand that your child may experience immediate relief from lying but at the same time may feel shame about having lied.

7. Don't label your child a liar. It will serve no purpose and may set up a self-fulfilling prophecy.

8. Embrace your child when she admits that she has lied or that telling the truth was hard.

9. Challenge the lie more than the person by saying, "I'm having a really hard time believing that story."

10. Get at the motivation behind the lie and don't give up until you find it.

11. Don't communicate that the lie is a threat to your relationship.

12. Prepare yourself for more conversations about the meaning of truth and honor.

Managing Fashion, Hip-Hop, and Offensive Language

Perhaps one of the biggest struggles for Black parents is how much to allow your children to identify with the cultural hip-hop tradition. Sometimes it seems overwhelming, like a tidal wave that you can't stop no matter how many times you say, "I brought you into this world, and I can take you out!" Preteens find identity development in music, fashion, and language in such a way that it's hard to avoid using music videos as the "Bible" of fashion and social conversation. Cursing has become punctuation in the language of teens, adults, popular culture, and society so much that sometimes people think you are speaking Greek if you don't use a four-letter word. It's hard for parents who were raised in homes where cursing was not allowed to tolerate any level of style that seems offensive. Fighting fashion has happened for centuries between parents and preteens, so don't feel that you are alone.

Our recommendation for managing fashion and popular culture is to develop standards that you will not go beyond and reasons why you won't go beyond them. Explain these rules and reasons to your child repeatedly from childhood through adolescence. Children and preteens can follow their parents' rules while desiring to be a part of popular culture. In fact, if you remember back, you probably did it too.

Please remember to get in the habit of saying no to buying material possessions or the right type of jeans for the sake of having the latest thing. Don't just give in to the pressure. Practice it when you are away from your child, because you know you are weak in their presence. Your defenses can break down. So practice saying no, especially when your child is expressing desperation with the desire ("I have to have these jeans, or I will die" or "I have to buy those shoes, or my friends will not like me"). Please also remember to follow "No" with a rationale like "I don't want you to grow up and not be your own person, and no one needs to have material things to be somebody." Another response is "I cannot support your thinking that who you are is what you wear." Sometimes our commentary along with the correction is the only antidote we have to the tidal wave of popular culture. It's not all bad. But know what you want your child to have. Set clear limits, with reasons as to why, and apply consequences when these limits are violated. And don't forget to whisper, "I want you to grow up and be your own person."

WATCHIN' OVER: PROTECTION WHEN WE ARE NOT AROUND

∽

One tree receiving all the wind breaks.

∽

Some of us grew up in a neighborhood where other people besides our immediate family constantly watched our behaviors and attitudes. We can remember "acting a fool" in a friend's house or backyard, only to have another adult discipline or speak to us as if they were our parent. As adolescence was beginning, these extra eyes watchin' over us were helpful when we decided to take risks that could end in danger. We want to emphasize how single or dual parenting is inadequate to protect our youth and to enable them to develop the necessary competence to succeed in today's hostile world. In fact, it is imperative that parents and families increase the number of positive relationships with other adults and role models so that children will feel empowered to exercise their God-given talents.

If you accept this community definition of discipline, then an absent parent or adult who tries to punish a child without first establishing a meaningful relationship will not see positive outcomes. This is not meaningful discipline. As we have mentioned earlier, discipline is not punishment. Effective discipline comes from a combination of affection, protection, and correction strategies that result in personal and extended self-awareness on the part of children, families, and communities of African descent. It involves a set of parent-child, neighbor-child, and community-family relationships in which praise and punishment go together. If "tough love" is to be heartfelt and useful, it must not be distinct from nurturance, or "soft love." Sometimes the toughest love is the parent's decision to provide tough and soft love simultaneously and to find others who can continue the strategies of affection, protection, and correction when the parent is not there. Discipline happens in a context where cultural values and rules are a major factor.

Howard Stevenson tells a story of his childhood that describes how communities can become villages to correct the behavior of youth. When Howard was a preteen growing up in rural southern Delaware, his parents gave him a bicycle for Christmas. Although he loved to ride his bike, it was not as much fun to do so on grass and rubble. Living in the country, in "the woods," you really appreciate "blacktop" (paved roads) because of the ease of riding on it. So there was always the desire to "ride on the road."

However, his family lived in a neighborhood with a road that stretched about a quarter of a mile with two sharp curves at either end. His parents would not let him ride on the road because it was too dangerous. All of his friends were able to ride on the blacktop, but he, his brother, and his sister felt trapped in their front yard, left to drool as their friends taunted them from the blacktop, performing daring bicycle tricks. To be teased by your friends is a fate worse than death to a preteen. Howard thought to himself, "I have to get to the blacktop!"

Well, one day he decided to disobey his parents, follow his dreams, and end his humiliation. He rode and performed wheelies and cartwheels and whatever else a twelve-year-old could do on a bicycle on the blacktop; and this bliss went on uninterrupted for three days. By the third day he had become Mario Andretti and would make circles in the road without turning to look back. Wouldn't you know that on this day while he was riding his bike on the blacktop and making a circle, not looking back, a car happened to be heading straight for him. At the last second, instead of hitting Howard, the car swerved and just barely tapped a tree. Howard rode as fast as he could home, hoping that he was not seen by the driver. As he looked back, he could see the man was not hurt but very shaken up.

Two days later the fear of being found out had worn off, and Howard could hear the blacktop calling, "Come!" The night before he planned to go out again, the car that almost hit him drove up into the driveway. His heart started beating so fast that the only noise he could make was that choking sound you get when your heart leaps up into your throat. A man of small stature and similar in age to Howard's father came to the door, asking to speak to "Hobby." Hobby was Howard's father's nickname among his close friends. It so happened that Howard's father and he had gone to the same school as children. What luck! What bad luck!

This man spoke to Howard's father and told him what had happened. The man felt obligated to tell Howard's father that Howard had almost been killed the other day. For Howard everything became a blur after that. Once Howard woke up from fainting and realized that he was not dreaming, his voice miraculously returned, and he confessed to being tempted by the blacktop. The discipline was just and swift. The rest is history. But from that day on, Howard believed that his father had eyes all over the place.

You must realize that discipline in this example includes Watchin' Over. Howard's punishment was only the consequence. The discipline involved the whole experience of being aware of misbehavior, anticipating being found out, fearing the potential consequences, and having older community members take responsibility for his misbehavior.

As African and biracial Americans, we must realize the virtue of our children having multiple parents. These "village" relationships have some very positive consequences for our children because there is no greater learning than that which comes from a caring relationship. Without a relationship all the material possessions in the world will not help children to know themselves, who they are, or where they came from. Positive contact with many adults and role models increases the chances that children and teenagers will learn how to appreciate their different identities and answer the following questions: Who am I? Who are my people? What does it mean to be male or female? What does it mean to be a son or daughter?

A lot of adults in Howard's community acted like fathers and mothers. These "uncles and aunts" had all the rights and privileges of parenthood. (This included spanking, although it rarely happened, thank God! But you believed it could happen at any point.) These practices still exist in many African American communities in the inner city and rural areas today. Some researchers call this "neighborhood social capital." It is a good thing. Teenagers often believe this Watchin' Over is painful because they are trying to figure out their identities, and having other people watch them is the ultimate adolescent nightmare—*no privacy!*

Although all that nosiness may bother children, and teenagers especially, it still has very far-reaching positive consequences. Research has found that cohesive neighborhoods have less crime and are safer neighborhoods. Drug dealers and burglars do not like to operate in places where they will be seen. Howard Stevenson has also found that Black youth who live in cohesive neighborhoods report lower levels of depression than Black youth who live in noncohesive neighborhoods. Being nosy can be a good thing if it saves the lives of children. It is a wonderful thing if it helps to reduce the stress that parents feel when raising children by themselves. Where it exists, Watchin' Over is very important to the lives of Black preteens who are beginning to test the limits of their world.

Remember Gary and Sheila and their son, Ahmad, whom we mentioned earlier? *Gary and Sheila do not have to culturally teach Ahmad how to survive and grow by themselves.* In fact, research finds that African American children who live in neighborhoods where adults know their families, their activities, their comings and goings, and their names feel safer than children who don't live in those types of neighborhoods. It means that by knowing you, others are likely to look out for your best interests and respond if you need help. If Gary and Sheila can marshal the resources in their community and invite trustworthy neighbors to help them parent Ahmad, they can increase Ahmad's opportunities for learning about himself, his culture, and the world.

We need to return to these types of relationships. Parents, single or dual, require multiple eyes on their children's lives, attitudes, and interactions. It may feel intrusive to a teenager to have every move questioned, so it is up to a parent when and how to relax the pressure. But in times of crisis children and youth need multiple adults to rely on, especially as many Black parents have to take one or two jobs just to make ends meet. Discipline begins with this communal perspective, with many eyes.

Applying effective consequences flows from the larger context of loving—not from revenge, life stress, hatred of young people, or frustration at a racist world. Parents would do well to identify several trustworthy neighbors who would commit to watching over their children when they are not around. This type of protection does not require a lot of effort, but it does require a common belief in unity.

Over time children and teenagers will look back on these experiences as necessary for their survival. The benefit of many eyes watching is not simply that children will be safer. It's also wonderful to have other adults show interest in the activities that children participate in. It means that there are many more people who can praise our children for "doing the right thing" or being competent in school or play.

The COPE Projects

Over the last ten years the authors of this book have led several parent empowerment projects called Community Outreach Through Parent Empowerment (COPE). In the COPE groups parents have lots of freedom and support to talk about their life aspirations and stressors in culturally relevant ways because that's what children deserve and want. By being able to talk about their life in the language and behavioral style they would use around their dinner table at home, parents feel "at home" in these groups and more comfortable to share fears and pain. Giving this cultural space to the parents encourages them to give the same to their children.

Many of the COPE groups include grandparents who are raising their grandchildren, and teenage parents who are struggling with their firstborn while living with their own parents. Amazingly enough, the teenage mothers will tell how their parents are overbearing, and then the grandparents in the group will explain what it's like to be a grandparent. It's fascinating to watch the teens listen to the older parents. Sometimes these "grandparents" become consultants and can tell the teens the very same things the teens' parents tell them. But in this setting the teens don't feel the same pressures they would feel with their own parents and find it easier to apply this wisdom. Even in the COPE groups it is possible to raise a village, with each person in the group helping others, which also means that the group leaders are not the only helpers.

In a village of caring adults, children have available a natural "posse" to protect them when danger occurs. *Posse* is a slang term for a group of friends who "watch your back." To have a community where other adults become extra parents or extra eyes and ears for us is a blessing. We feel that parents who do not have this don't have to remain isolated. This is especially true for single parents, who, like two parents, need as much support as they can get! The key is for parents to establish smaller villages in order to keep their children protected.

Howard remains grateful to that man who thought enough of him and his family to go out of his way to tell Howard's father what had happened. Although painful at the time, community protection is like having one big invisible security blanket!

In the next chapter, we will address how African American parents can prepare their teenage children with a posse, a village, and a lot of prayer.

5

When Black Children Fly, the World Retaliates

Self-Discipline for the Teenager

Parenting is a lifelong acquaintance with helplessness.

My mother grew up in north Philadelphia, and my father grew up in southern Delaware. Both were African American, but their cultures were as different as New York City is from Beirut. I grew up in a multicultural household. One major difference was in their styles of managing racial conflict. My father's style was much more laid back and didn't focus on race as a conflict of importance. He usually wanted to avoid conflicts, believing God would take care of racist people in the end. My mother was more challenging, like Malcolm X, or at least the caricature of him. She would not let White people treat her any ol' way without a fight. And if I, my brother, or sister was treated unfairly, there would be war. No fists, but when she got through telling them about themselves and their families, and the injustices of racism in the world, the racist teacher, policeman, or candlestick maker would feel knocked down to the ground. All that would be needed was for someone to come and take the bodies away. Then she would pray for them.

Howard Stevenson

∿

Throughout this chapter we will combine the three ingredients of effective discipline because as adolescents develop, parents are often providing affection, protection, and correction in the same actions. Developmentally, it makes sense to see these three elements of discipline in everything we say and do with teens, because they are sensitive watchers and screeners of everything we do. Practically, it's hard to pull off well.

STICKIN' TO, WATCHIN' OVER, AND GETTIN' WITH YOUR TEENAGER: PRAYING YOUR TEEN WILL MAKE GOOD DECISIONS

In Chapter Four we recommended nurturing your preteen from a short distance. Some of those same rules apply for teenagers, except that now you have even less control. That's why prayer is a valid recourse. It's a valid recourse from the cradle to the grave, but adolescence has a special way of bringing parents to their knees. Parental helplessness is often at its highest point during a child's adolescence. At no point in life is the need for independence in the child challenging the parental fear of tragedy and need for control so strongly.

Praying to your Creator, contemplating, or simply meditating allows you to recognize that you don't control as much as you think. Reliance on a higher being can clear your mind of worry so that you can hear your child's unspoken feelings, reach back and grab the wisdom of self, family, and culture, and make better decisions. Discipline requires an appreciation of spirituality because sometimes the world is larger than our wisdom, our reach, our worry. There is a famous song in the Black church called "Somebody Bigger Than You and I," and it reminds us that the world was created by forces larger than ourselves, so worrying about daily unpredictable occurrences is futile.

Psychologically, adolescence raises more worry, especially if our own teen years were difficult. Research has found that reliance on a spiritual source can reduce anxiety, increase relaxation, and promote mental and physical health for African Americans from childhood to old age. Teenagers are also going to need this same source—because they are beginning to question the meaning of life. Lead by example. Your self-discipline can represent a strategy they can borrow in times of crisis. And, yes, there will be crises from within your teen's spirit and from without.

What Is the Meaning of Life?

The meaning of life becomes a more substantial concern for teenagers. Preteens respond to the negotiation of a hug. Teenagers begin to question the foundational reason for the existence of nurturance. Now teens ask, "Why do you need to hug me?" or "What is the meaning of a hug?"

For families who have raised their children in a religious or spiritual environment, these adolescent dilemmas of meaning can be understood better but not entirely. If these environments appreciate the unique developmental, cultural, and contemporary needs of Black youth, then teens will have more resources to carry with them on their journey in search of truth.

Teachers and institutions that are culturally and developmentally relevant can be excellent guides along this search for identity. These individuals and institutions still must come under the ever questioning eye of the teen, who needs to reevaluate all things in his life, including the pastor or imam. But if parents, teachers, and religious institutions are barriers in this search for identity and truth, they risk becoming irrelevant, meaningless, and of no use to the teenager's identity development.

Character Is Self-Discipline

Self-respect, self-reliance, and the development of identity are the hallmarks of teenage life. The passion for and meaning of certain world causes are often attached to the teenager's personal search for identity, freedom, and truth. It's time now for your "baby" to try to fly. This is the making of character.

Preteens have been growing wings. Teenagers try to use them. Preteens rebel out of a newfound curiosity for exploration. Adolescents rebel out of a desperate search for truth. This resistance takes on a whole new twist. So to fulfill the mandate of effective Black parenting and discipline for teenagers, parents have to consider how their affection, protection, and correction will *aid* the teenager in his search for identity.

A wonderful irony of adolescence is that childhood memories and the example set by parents and older siblings as they manage life stressors daily are the foundation for the decisions adolescents will make to prove to the world that they have an identity. Without strong adult role models, teens are left to make important life decisions about things like sexual behavior and rejecting trouble, by themselves or based on the advice of other inexperienced teens. Teen advice is sometimes useful, sometimes lacking, and usually based on limited experience. Most of the time it's like "the blind leading the blind." The influence of family, friends, culture, and personality all seem to be visible in the behaviors of the adolescent, for better or worse. But we focus on the need for discipline for Black youth because of the unique challenges they face in a world of limited opportunity.

In the story at the beginning of this chapter, Howard Stevenson remembers his parents' styles of managing racial injustice and conflict as part of the ways in which his own adolescence took shape. Adolescents borrow from their parents' ways of reacting to difficult situations. A subtle but powerful form of discipline comes from the values that Black parents and family leaders live by on a daily basis. How parents manage racial identity, difficulties, or relationships will teach a youth about how to manage the complexities of life.

Black youth can make decisions about social and personal injustice by remembering what their parents do and used to do. It's amazing how these strategies come to mind under stress. And stress is a major experience of adolescence too. But these stressful experiences often develop restraint, denial, or protest (or some combination of these) in the Black teen who seeks to make a mark on the world. At the least, it develops character.

Margaret Spencer, a leading child developmental psychologist, has studied the dynamics of how social status, neighborhoods, culture, and coping strategies affect the identity and character of Black youth. She and her colleagues have found that "identity is coping" and often what we see in youth are behaviors that represent the identity of the struggling adolescent (Spencer, Cunningham, and Swanson, 1995). The teenager is trying to make meaning of the world and herself through her behaviors. So whereas "being" (who I will be someday) is helping to develop identity, "doing" (what I do now is who I am) is about identity as coping. What teens do in the moment helps to create meaning for them and is part of answering the meaning-of-life question.

Another aspect of adolescent identity development that is hard for parents is that although teens don't necessarily know who they are, they can begin to say who they are not. And often parents are the target of this "identity-by-elimination" process. Teens seem to say, "I may not know who I am, but at least I'm not my dad [or mom]." This will certainly change once teens grow to be young adults and have children of their own, when that mad rush of memory will hit them and they will scream, "Oh, that's exactly what my father used to say!" But until then parents are the identity punching bags of teens trying to make sense of themselves. Don't lose hope. This is all still about the teen developing character—his, not yours.

Character could be another word for self-discipline. Teenagers are beginning to learn the meaning of self-discipline and when, why, and how to apply it. Discipline for the adolescent must still encompass affection, protection, and correction, but parents must adjust by watching how their teenager is becoming her own person. We must encourage and pray that she will affect, protect, and correct herself. We will begin to witness the fruit of our labor up to this point as well as watch how the "grown child" begins to shape herself. A little adult is about to emerge, and not only do the rules change but so do the consequences.

The Social Images and Consequences of Being a Black Teenager

"Image is everything," touts a young Andre Agassi in a commercial about cameras, and nothing could be closer to the truth for Black youth. The incarceration rate of Black teens in America is high, and higher than for White youth who commit the same crimes. Black males are two times more likely to be arrested and seven times more likely to be held in detention facilities than White youth are (Snyder and Sickmund, 1999). Black youth abuse drugs and alcohol less than White youth, yet you would never know it from watching the six o'clock news or reading the daily newspaper. In a study conducted by the Annenberg School of Communication at the University of Pennsylvania (Romer, Jamieson, and de Coteau, 1998), researchers found that the coverage of crime by African Americans on the three major news channels in one U.S. city was significantly greater than the percentage of actual crime committed by African Americans. These images create false assumptions about the magnitude of social ills in our community while minimizing the extent of these ills in other neighborhoods.

In our society, if you go to court, you are innocent until proven guilty. However, many Black families believe that in the court of public opinion (the media), if you are Black, you are considered to be *guilty*—with or without a court, a trial, or even evidence. This is what Amos Wilson (1990), in his book *Black-on-Black Violence: The Psychodynamics of Black Self-Annihilation in Service of White Domination*, calls "cosmically guilty." He says that Black males in particular are thought of as problematic simply because of their status and presence as Black males.

So stickin' to, watchin' over, and gettin' with teenagers has to accomplish two things. One, as we have stated, is that it must help teens reach a secure sense of personal, gender, and racial identity. Second, it must address the social tendency to stigmatize African American youth culture, behavior, and potential.

> ### Stressors Black Teenagers Have to Face
>
> 1. Expectations of intellectual inferiority and lack of world knowledge
> 2. Expectations and fears of aggressive and hostile intent and behavior
> 3. Expectations and fears of sexually promiscuous behavior
> 4. Expectations of criminality and "cosmic guilt"

"At Least I Got My Child to Eighteen!"

∽

Child, I am so glad that boy graduated from high school, I don't know what to do. Not everybody can say that, with all these kids out here dropping like flies. He's not on the corner, and he's alive. I've done my job.

Rashida, age thirty-nine, mother, Philadelphia

∽

Many parents of Black youth have the challenge and fear that while their children are still youth, the world may see them as grown men and women. Over the years, many parents in our parenting programs have told us that they are so thankful to be able to say, "At least I got my child to eighteen!" The reason is that so many parents see adolescence as the most dangerous time of a Black youth's life.

Homicide is the leading cause of death for Black youth in both urban and rural environments. When you mix ageism (injustices and discrimination against young people or elderly) with racism, Black youth experience a double or triple whammy—a status that can put them in jeopardy every day. As we have said previously, there is a window of opportunity for some youth, but for Black youth the opportunity is more like a crack in the window.

That being said, there is no reason for us to assume that just because Black teenagers are Black, they understand the life implications of such a social status.

Being Black Doesn't Mean Understanding Blackness

Many Black youth do not understand the larger racial, social, and aspirational implications of being Black in America. But adolescence is the beginning of deeper-level thinking, and it is possible for them to begin to understand the implications of one's social status in the world. They can begin to understand the systemic nature of racism. But only if they are taught.

If taught, the Black adolescent can begin to understand not only that Blacks get treated unfairly sometimes but that this problem happens in a systemic fashion. They can learn how racism influences hiring, firing, and a host of attitudes on the part of personnel in public establishments. They can begin to make sense of why police and ambulances come faster in neighborhoods of Whites and wealthy constituents when there is an emergency and how this reality can affect their daily lives. They can begin to realize how "driving while Black" is more than a punch line to a joke. But someone has to teach them. Although it has been said that "parents are the first teachers," in the matter of race, children are the last to know.

The Bomb Squad

A host of racial issues take on greater significance when adolescence kicks in. But there have to be guides to point out the deeper meaning of these situations. Without a guide the search for truth and identity will remain intense but superficial.

We are advocating that during the teenage years discipline for Black youth has to include parents who deeply understand the importance of teaching their teens what it means to be Black, with all of its triumphs and tribulations. Why? Because now teens are confronting experiences that will cause them to pause, listen, and react in ways they were developmentally unable to before. And if your fifteen-year-old is a child in your eyes but perceived as an aggressive adult in the eyes of society, shouldn't you be the one to tell them what to do about this gross injustice? Parents cannot leave their teens to fend for themselves, despite teens' protesting, "Leave me alone!" The world is a minefield for Black youth; parents, family, communities, and villages must be the bomb squad.

So how do you provide affection, correction, and protection under these life circumstances? Pray every day.

To Be Uncool Is to Die

To a teenager irrelevance is death. Erik Erickson, the famous developmental psychologist, was quoted as saying, "A bad identity is better than no identity at all." Everyone needs to be known for something. In our society "cool" is how you become relevant. It was just as true in your adolescence as it is now. You know it was. You just forgot (or wanted to forget or blocked it out due to severe traumatic breach). The big difference today is that cool as a lifestyle has become a moneymaking vehicle of gigantic proportions.

Being cool is the drug of American youth pop culture, and there are many dealers ready to hand out the next new thing that will make youth cool. In an article on Black youth adjustment in junior high schools, Stanlaw and Peshkin (1988) remark that "being cool is not a way of life for teenagers, it is life." Individual cool—not culture, spirituality, heritage, or family—has become the new content of one's character.

So Black youth, like any other youth, have to find some way to be cool. Some become "cool addicts." Fashion, music, and language are the major vehicles for expressing cool. You must represent something, be somebody, in order to exist. For adults existence and being somebody can happen at the same time. For adolescents, being somebody special comes before existence is possible. Be cool first, and identity will come later, right? *Wrong!*

How to Know If Your Black Teen Is Cool Addicted

1. She advocates that grunting and head movements should become a secondary language.

2. He walks, moves, and responds to conversation as slowly as possible.

3. She argues that you as a parent "stress too much."

4. He argues with you to the death about the importance of being his own person, and then you have a hard time picking him out of a crowd after sports practice because all of his friends are wearing the exact same "unique" pair of baggy jeans, hoodie, and sneaks.

5. Whining, yelling, and spastic temper tantrums stop the moment other teens enter the premises.

6. The music he listens to includes "new, unheard-of" four-letter-word phrases.

7. She takes more than a minute to explain to you what cool is.

8. Your nickname is "Oldhead."

Never before has cool been for sale for so much. On playgrounds at school and in school classrooms, the verbal art of "playing the dozens" has been transformed into trash-talking about another child's lack of style or lack of cool. Instead of showing off one's ability to handle verbal challenges, which was the goal of playing the dozens, this trash-talking leads to fights.

Discipline that involves affection must act as a "snitch" and disclose daily the falsity of this notion of cool. The affection of Black folk must say to Black teens today, "You only think cool is identity, but it's really a trap." Cool is a trap because everybody wants it. Cool sells cigarettes, it sells liquor, it sells success. Cool is instant success. In *Cool Pose: The Dilemmas of Black Manhood in America*, Richard Majors and Janet Billson (1992) write about how cool helps young Black males to defend themselves against a society that seeks to find fault with, attack, and humiliate them. By being cool, one can protect oneself.

If we apply the both-and concept to cool, we can see that on one hand, it may be protective but that on the other hand, it offers little substance to help teens develop a real sense of self. The positive aspect of cool is that it teaches adolescents what the world considers to be relevant. The negative effects of cool can lead to self-destruction. Cool doesn't develop identity; it only mimics it. Cool may provide some level of protection, but it's flimsy protection; and it can't provide affection or correction to developing bodies, minds, and souls. Cool involves pretending to be something teens are not. Constant exposure to cool without discipline can lead to what we call "hypervulnerability."

Hypervulnerability

Understanding cool is important to understanding how Black adolescents develop identity. But understanding what happens when adolescents rely way too much on cool instead of substance is also important. In our research we have found that hypervulnerability among some Black youth is a very valuable phenomenon to witness.

Hypervulnerability is a tendency

1. To feel consistently that you are not cared for by loving family or friends

2. To expect comments about one's behavior, dress, or person to be hurtful attacks

3. To feel insecure on the inside and defend one's insecurity at all costs, sometimes at great risk to one's safety

4. To "fight first and ask questions later," or to attack others before they attack

5. To get swallowed up in the negative aspects of being cool and fail to experience protection, affection, and correction

6. To feel that defending one's dignity is more important than life

7. To want caring from others but having few emotional resources to express that

8. To receive caring if others take the first step, see your insecurity and fears, and provide open arms instead of attacking

Hypervulnerability can be contagious unless intervention identifies the symptoms of hypervulnerability and stops the cycle.

Hypervulnerability happens when youth rely heavily on empty realities (like being cool at all costs) to develop their sense of self. It also occurs when protection, affection, and correction are not available in equal intensity. Without a consistency of discipline, many Black youth feel insecure and do not expect safety, caring, and accountability to come for them.

The "art" of trash-talking is common among many teenagers. Trash-talking is when folks get together and boast about their own abilities and skills while putting down the skills of others. It becomes more problematic in social relationships when there are crowds of peers who egg on or instigate others to trash-talk against each other or even cheer the best trash-talker. Some have called it "busting" or "playing the dozens" or "snapping." Often, trash-talking is a demonstration of cool. For example, someone might say, "Your mother is so poor, she can't even pay attention." That's an older version of someone saying, "Your mother told me you wet the bed. In fact, I was in her bed last night when she told me."

Trash-talking becomes more hurtful if you don't have a strong sense of identity, history, and future. At the core of a lot of trash-talking is the humiliation of the self—somebody else's self. Sometimes teens trash-talk in order not to be the one who gets talked about. Under these circumstances youth will want to get back at the assailant or lash out at the world for not providing their basic needs. When some youth have not received all three ingredients of discipline—affection, protection, and correction—they feel more justified in fighting to survive. Without a sense of nurturance, safety, and ethical behavior, you may fight just to feel good. If words, style, and fashion make up your identity, anything someone says about you will feel like a whuppin', and your greatest tendency will be to whup back. In reality, both parents and youth can suffer from hypervulnerability, and sometimes it can ruin our relationships.

Countering Cool

Cool is like a signpost. Although it can alert you to a number of directions, it doesn't tell you which are the best roads to take. So parents have to learn how to counter cool.

One way parents can do this is to let cool rub off on them. Teens need affection, which must come consistently. Maybe you can't hug him in public, but you can learn the latest handshakes that reflect cool and still communicate "I love you" to him. In the mind of your adolescent, it may reflect something much more contemporary: "I love you, Homie [or "Dogg" or "Man"—or whatever the contemporary slang is for *best friend*]."

Be interested in your teenager's language and personal way of trying to be cool. Ask questions and act like a novice about their world (because you are). Ask about the music and the lyrics. This can communicate affection without preaching. Teens hate preaching, but that is no reason to stop doing it. Just balance the preaching with the listening type of affection that says, "Who you are becoming is very interesting to me. I may be scared about it, but I will be here for you from the beginning of the metamorphosis to the end."

One way to provide developmentally appropriate CPR for teens is to ask them to critique the lyrics of some of their rap music instead of just passively accepting them. Just like we recommended that you become a commentator on what your younger children watch on TV, we recommend that you comment on the lyrics that teens listen to and ask how committed they are to them. Most of these discussions can trigger deeper-level discussions about meaning and can also support a student's newfound skills of argumentation. This is what psychologists like Roderick Watts and Jaleel Abdul-Adil (1997) and Janie Victoria Ward (1996) call "critical consciousness raising" in Black boys and girls, where the goal is to increase in the individual a propensity to challenge culturally irrelevant and alienating influences.

These discussions with Black youth are essential to helping them affirm what they know and what they believe because it has been taken through "the fire" of debate. Often parents will be relieved and surprised at how much their teenagers espouse values similar to those of their parents and at how much they disagree with the popular culture that undermines those values—even if they listen to the music. But parents would never find that out without this kind of conversation.

So ask them to teach you, and then teach them by making them defend their involvement in something. This is a form of discipline that fits well within our view of Stickin' To, because you are in a relationship with your child as you challenge them to defend their views. It's age appropriate, but it has the potential to develop a set of standards and values that he or she will apply when you are not around. And frankly, parents are rarely around when adolescents need to make difficult social and personal decisions. So if you can't be there twenty-four–seven (that's twenty-four hours a day, seven days a week for those who don't know the lingo), challenging their values in a caring way is the next best thing. Let the cool rub off on you.

Our concept of how to manage hypervulnerability involves identifying the racial and cultural traps in society, providing CPR to Black youth on a regular and consistent basis, and applying the three ingredients of discipline. It is not always possible for all three ingredients to be equally distributed. This can heighten hypervulnerability. Some kids have family experiences where the affection is there, but the correction and protection are lacking. Some kids have families where the correction and protection are the strongest theme, but affection is invisible. These different combinations lead to more hypervulnerability in youth as well as to the desire to defend oneself "at all costs."

Sometimes, socially conscious television shows and movies can demonstrate the kind of behaviors and interactions that can help youth manage their hypervulnerability. *Boys from the Hood* is a movie that reflects the urban life of many Black youth, who struggle with gender and cultural identity development, violence, parenting, and survival. One of the main characters, Trey, learns how to resist temptations by holding on to his father's teachings about life, which mostly involved teaching about the dangers of being a Black person in a racist society. Laurence Fishburne, playing Furious Styles, the father of Trey, was someone who held his ground on the importance of "doing the right thing" and on what it means to be a real Black man. In the role, he demonstrated some strong affection, but his character was stronger in skills of CPR, protection, and correction. Trey was struggling through the challenge, faced by many Black males, of making decisions for himself while injustice and tragedy pull him away from personal goals. Styles is a wonderful example of a parent trying to balance all three ingredients of discipline in a world that keeps Black youth in a "damned if you do, damned if you don't" position.

Unfortunately, "catch-22" doesn't fully describe the situation of Black teenagers, and this is why we have advocated that Black youth and parents engage in and experience "catch-33."

Understanding the Catch-33

Preparing African American teens for survival in an environment that may act malevolently toward them requires families to balance explanations of harsh realities with hopeful messages of opportunity. In reality, the earlier we start preparing them, the better. Adolescence is too late to start the conversation on race, but it's the time the need for this conversation becomes greater. Some suggest that the dilemma of whether or not to discuss race with children is a "damned if you do, damned if you don't" situation—what many people call a "catch-22."

However, we believe the catch-22 dilemma is different and too simple to explain the trauma of racism for African Americans. To us catch-22 is situational and temporary and represents singular, isolated incidents of psychological assault. So when acts of racism occur, our natural human inclination is to judge them based on the particular situation. The dilemma is that if you make one decision, you are in hot water, and if you make the opposite decision, you are still in hot water.

One example is whether or not to believe racism is a reality that requires us as parents to prepare our children to deal with it. Many parents fear that if you do prepare them, you will contribute to a paranoia that serves no positive purpose for the child. Some fear it could create hostility in the child, who may anticipate danger where little exists. If you decide not to talk about these issues, could your child be unprepared for the psychological assaults of racist acts that gnaw at children's self-esteem daily? Still, both sides of this dilemma are usually based on a belief that you raise these issues a lot or a little because of potential single acts of racism.

The catch-33

---

1. Is not "damned if you do, damned if you don't" but, rather, "just damned by society"

> 2. Is when one sees that catch-22 racist situations are not isolated but systemic and one can no longer deny this tragedy
>
> 3. Is a situation that requires CPR and village strategies to combat it

Unfortunately, we believe there is a third psychological dilemma and that catch-22 does not fully capture: the long-term effects of being in multiple "damned if you do, damned if you don't" situations. Catch-33 represents the struggle to adopt the belief that one or one's people are "just damned" (only in the eyes of society). Catch-33 represents the larger tragedy of facing the reality that this catch-22 situation is historic and structural and may not change. It is the inability to explain why these situations are not isolated. It doesn't matter how smart you are, how much education you have, how much money you have—these situations continue regardless. The psychological assault did not just occur once or yesterday.

Sometimes it is hard to watch young African Americans realize for the first time, say in college, that they are being discriminated against. It brings a certain "dis-ease" of spirit when you know that your abilities are questioned simply because of your skin color. It's like that feeling of instability folks get within their soul after an earthquake. You do not really know whether the steps you take are going to be as sure as you've always expected them to be. Once we surmise that it is not the particularities of the insults (for example, a racist and ignorant assailant or hate group) but a larger system, it may shock us to learn that the "damned if you do, damned if you don't" dilemma is not momentary, isolated, and temporary, like the mumps or measles. This then is a tragedy, is it not?

When a Black teenager (with no gun) is shot (multiple times) by police officers for no reason, shot in the back (and it is described as self-defense), or hung in his cell (with no apparent suicidal ideation or history), it is one thing. But when things like this happen again and again and again, with no forceful challenge to their absurdity, horror, or repetition, it is something altogether different and tragic. That is the catch-33—the sneaking feeling that catch-22 dilemmas are infinite and will continue. This is where the trauma of being Black can feel like psychological assault. Amazingly enough, some African Americans don't experience this until adulthood, but it is our belief that the teen years are often when the struggle for the meaning of life is open to discovering, understanding, and becoming traumatized by the catch-33.

If racism is systemic and not situational, then one cannot simply get out of the dilemma by himself and expect the matter to be done with. One must confront the psychological assault in its larger context in order to combat and sidestep the catch-33.

Combating the Catch-33

Facing this tragedy constitutes a higher-order sense of anomie that is not remedied by one's effort, one's psychological coping talents, skills, or development, or one's accomplishments. In the same way that influencing or avoiding the random acts or "bad" people will not prevent or limit the onslaught of racism trauma, one's effort becomes inadequate. Such a situation can lead to what Cornell West (1993) calls "nihilism," the very loss of hope (Stevenson, 1998b).

What parents can do about this potential loss of hope is CPR. When you think about it, tears are probably the healthiest response one can react with. By definition, to try and solve this hopelessness on one's own is to fail because it takes a village, a community, a posse to address it (Stevenson, 1998a). We propose that proactive and protective CPR is necessary to counteract the belittling expectations of the catch-33.

In order to sidestep the catch-33, one must have access to ways of thinking above and beyond the current dilemmas of why society fears Black folk, and Black youth in particular. Parents must examine that fear and teach youth that they don't have to adopt it for themselves. This is where "somebody bigger than you and I" can help. A spiritual reality for inspiration, a cultural heritage for root-edness, and an appreciation of the extended self for companionship are needed to combat the catch-33 and make sense of the loss of hope and the apathy that are expected in catch-33 politics.

How to Resolve the Catch-33

1. Acknowledge that racism is based on fear.

2. Realize that to react to racism in unhealthy ways means accepting this fear.

3. Get CPR in protective and proactive ways for yourself and learn how to focus on the culture, not the oppression; the system, not the situation; the triumph, not the tragedy.

4. Use spiritual resources because they provide sustenance that reduces worry over catch-33 events that we have no control over.

5. Create a village of people you can trust to provide CPR when you are not around.

6. Teach your children steps 1–5.

What can we do about the potential for catch-33 apathy? One thing is to believe that rugged individualism does not work for build-ing healthy relationships. We propose that it takes a village to raise a child, a teenager, an adult, an elder, a family, and everyone else in between—from the cradle to the grave. Ultimately, the CPR, or cul-tural socialization, that we propose can teach youth how to inter-pret the systemic nature of racism and how not to get sucked into it. It's not just thinking—it's thinking about how to feel and con-sidering one's thinking. It's like the difference between being given fish to eat and learning how to fish for oneself. Eventually, youth can learn to resist systemic racism with confidence and deeper self-knowledge rather than reacting to it out of fear.

When Teens Feel Like Slaves

∽

Don't ask me where I am going; ask me where I have come from.

∽

Many of my friends, and now even my own children, ask me, "Why do you talk so much about slavery and the sixties? Those are the ol' days." Yes, this is the new millennium. But how will we move forward if we do not know our past? Should we forget the holocaust because it was ugly? Why should we forget our own history, as painful as it may be? We must never forget. How do we prepare our children for tomorrow if they do not know the mistakes of our yesterdays?

∽

Frequently Asked Questions

- How do I teach my child to like himself while I discipline him?

- I don't want him to feel like a slave, but sometimes he has to learn to listen. How do I get him to understand that?

The impact of oppression and historical enslavement on the larger negative image of African Americans has major implications for when we may belittle each other and our children. It is important to learn to talk to youth about this stark historical reality and yet give them meaning and hope. It's important for them to know the psychological and historical effects of enslavement—what happens to people when they are treated badly and how it can lead to treating your own loved ones badly.

In addition, we must seek freedom from an underlying sense of inferiority that has been ingrained in our psyche. As Bob Marley (1980) sings in "Redemption Song," "Let us free ourselves from mental slavery, none but ourselves can free our minds." As we have said in previous chapters, we must try to connect our own feelings of inferiority with those that we may unconsciously communicate to our children and that may re-create in them the same sense of timidity and fear.

Some parents are more comfortable parenting younger children than adolescents. The sense of rebellion in adolescents is harder to deal with, or maybe the parent's own adolescence was difficult. The unresolved emotions of a tormenting adolescence can make parenting an adolescent doubly hard. It is better to rely on those past experiences than to hide from them as if they will go away. They may just raise their ugly head when you become a parent; you know this is happening if the same feelings are being re-created. Talking about them minimizes their negative effects—it's like a vaccination against future negative effects.

∽

Do not borrow from the world, for the world will require its own back with interest.

∽

Dealing with the "System"

How can I keep my dignity and respect with these "system helpers" if they keep treating me like dirt? How can I protect my children and get these workers out of my life? How can I use the system to work for me instead of against me?

∽

Sometimes teenagers can engage in activities that bring their rebellion to the attention of social authorities. If this happens, families are, unfortunately, faced with having their family problems visible to social systems. Calling the cops on your child can be a difficult reality given the way the system responds to Black youth. Unfortunately, life makes these left, then backward, turns.

Often the fear is of the lack of concern that system helpers, or "White folk," have regarding African American culture, style, and behavior. "White people" does not always mean parents or people who are Caucasian; it also denotes social service systems. Physical discipline is often the topic when these discussions about race and systems take place. We think it is important to face the question of physical discipline (for example, spanking) head-on, not by scapegoating the parents who practice spanking. We want to say again that we do not condone the use of physical discipline in raising children. However, we want to explain why families use it and under what circumstances it may be helpful.

Our society expects every cultural group to parent the same way. Because American social systems often overlook cultural differences in parenting and family life, many social systems are paralyzed in their ability to help families of color. Often this results because these helpers cannot relate to the experiences that many parents in poor or culturally different neighborhoods go through. They suggest to African American parents that their forms of discipline are wrong. This manner of "telling Black folks how to raise their children" fails to appreciate the life struggles and strengths of Black people.

Often African American parents are faced with a timeless and historical catch-22 when receiving help from professionals (often European American but not always) who criticize parenting and family lifestyle first and ask questions later. This catch-22 is similar to the master-slave relationship: one person plays the role of uninformed "expert," and the family is expected to play the role of grateful servant. Once this dynamic rears its ugly head, the opportunity to discuss different forms of punishment is almost gone. This is because resistance on the part of Black parents to the European American strategy of "blaming the victim" is cultural and protective and kicks in at this time. The more we fight or defy an oppressive system or individual, the more we are engaging in the oldest form of African American expression—resistance against enslavement.

∽

Even though you may enter the house, you don't always enter the hearts.

∽

When poorly trained and culturally ignorant helpers stimulate this resistance behavior, the ability to rationally discuss parenting disappears. The helper may keep talking about parenting, but the Black family or parent has stopped listening! We train professionals to identify this cultural dynamic, to sidestep it, and to appreciate that resistance is necessary before one can develop culturally competent and empowering parenting techniques. Unfortunately, parent educators need training in understanding Black culture, context, and strengths and in how to get over their fears.

When the Police Don't Understand

Most police officers are caring individuals who protect and serve the public good. But research has found that Black youth are more likely than other youth to face harsher punishment and misinterpretation of behavior at the hands of police officers. We think parents have to be proactive about their conversations with youth.

Howard Stevenson remembers a conversation about police officers with his son, Bryan, when Bryan was nine years old:

HOWARD: Bryan, do you know what to do when a cop stops you or says something to you?

BRYAN: Yes—no—what do you mean?

HOWARD: I want you to remember to be polite even if the cop is rude to you.

BRYAN: Why? If he is mean to me, why should I be nice to him?

HOWARD: Because some cops—not all cops, but some cops— don't always care about you or know you to be the sweet, adorable boy that I know and love. Unfortunately, some cops think that Black boys are angry and aggressive and will fight them.

BRYAN: I wouldn't do that.

HOWARD: I know that, but sometimes some police don't know that. And they may be scared that you will fight them back. By being polite, saying, "No, sir" and "Yes, sir," and answering all of the questions he or she asks you, you may make the police officer less scared, less likely to hurt you, and more likely to treat you better.

BRYAN: That doesn't make sense. Why should I have to be going through all that?

HOWARD: Trust me, African Americans don't always get the same treatment, so I want you to be ready if it happens. If it doesn't happen, great! But if it does happen, I want you to be ready. Okay?

BRYAN: Okay.

HOWARD: Okay, let's go through it again. What do you do when a police officer or any authority figure stops you and starts to ask you questions?

Of course, when talking to teens, the conversation shifts, but we hope that you will start this conversation early even if teens are more likely to be targeted. We recommend that you have this type of conversation with your teenage boys and girls over and over and over again. It's almost exactly like the "stop, drop, and roll" conversation some parents have with their kids to explain what they should do if they find themselves in a fire. Give detailed, explicit instructions to your children through their teenage years, answer all questions, and apply the instructions to different types of situations.

The conversation is meant to prepare them, relax them, and alert them to the nonverbal unspoken dynamics of racism in everyday social interactions.

"Actin' the Fool" and Ending Up in Jail

To understand discipline among Black folk, it is important to understand the history of resistance. Resistance must be understood in a cultural context. In many instances parents discipline their children in order for them to behave in ways that do not bring more oppression on their children. The goal of a lot of Black parenting is to prepare children for a world that may seek to destroy their creativity and talent. Historically, Black folks have had to be the comedians, the entertainers, and the all-around court jesters for Whites, who could only tolerate Black talent within a narrow frame best described as "actin' the fool." Some believe those rules haven't changed. So disciplining children so that they don't "act the fool" in public is also meant to stop feeding into White racist expectations that Blacks are "easygoing," silly, and unintelligent.

cs

He who has not carried your burden does not know how much it weighs.

cs

Many African Americans feel that their children may face an unloving and unforgiving world. In the words of some Black parents, "It would be better that you learn from me how to handle hardship than from the world." Some parents will say, "Don't think you can get away with this behavior out there!" or "You can act like a fool here, but the moment you act up in school, in the street, or out there, they will put you in jail."

There are benefits and disadvantages to this thinking, and both must be understood. There are reasons for parenting in preparation for a harsh world, but if there is an overemphasis on protection and resistance, and an underemphasis on creativity and potential, children will suffer. This is part of the dilemma of being Black in America. What you can do is overshadowed and overlooked by powerful men and women who often don't believe you can do anything at all! One's potential can be dismissed if anything negative is observed. Potential becomes swallowed up in misperception. Discipline in Black families often becomes the mechanism by which we protect children from the pain of ongoing misperception. It may also be the way Black parents struggle through their pain of having their potential blocked or misperceived.

Through a form of self-denial, some Black folk are disgusted by behaviors that may "bring the race down." Some doors of opportunity are closed to Blacks if they behave without intense restraint. This self-denial and restraint are unfair and difficult because they mean that African Americans cannot outwardly express their full range of emotions and behaviors. This often forces us to swallow our anger—an anger based on feeling phony and being what the world expects Black folk to be. Some Black folk just refuse to "wear the mask"! And they should refuse, but with a posse in their corner, not alone.

✺

The lion's story will never be known as long as the hunter is the one to tell it.

✺

No Black Teen Is an Island

This concept of self-knowledge leads to another issue important to African American mental health—community survival. An undisciplined child or parent will not be able to discern how others are thinking of him or her. To be undisciplined is to be unaware of one's behavior when others are around. To be unaware of self in the context of others represents interpersonal retardation or isolation.

A healthy African American becomes so because the community (in the form of church groups, family reunions, Black student leagues, and so forth) around him or her is responsive, nurturing, and supervisory. And effective discipline becomes the vehicle by which children learn to be in community with others. Effective discipline teaches children how to define who the community is and how to help the community. It becomes the mechanism by which parents can reduce their isolated survival and get help with tough decisions. Such learning cannot take place fully if one is unaware of what many African American psychologists often call the "extended self."

Now is a good time to review the Haitian proverb quoted earlier. If we take community seriously, we should revise it to read, "If you want your eggs hatched, you have to sit on them with your extended self." *Self* in African American psychology is not defined as just "me, myself, and I." *Self* means being connected to key people in our lives: "you, them, and us." To be alone and unaware of my neighbor, my community, or my people is to risk being isolated, which often leads to pain, anger, and constant frustration.

Communication about the consequences of racial discrimination has to be more direct with adolescents. As children grow older, it becomes harder to shield them from the harshness and promote the beauty of being Black in America.

In Chapter Four we told you about Gary and Sheila, two African American parents dealing with multiple dilemmas in parenting their son, Ahmad. Gary and Sheila would go crazy if all they were concerned about was Ahmad's "aggressiveness." They know that many Whites, unfamiliar with African American culture and style, are likely to misinterpret Ahmad's behavior, and they want to protect against that. They also have experience with being perceived as hostile. But to focus only on "what Whites think of us" will lead Ahmad and his parents to a life of neurosis and paranoia.

"Beautiful Are the Souls of My People": Cultural Pride Reinforcement for the Teenager

Frequently Asked Questions

- Why should I talk to my child about culture?

- All this talk about Africa has nothing to do with living in Philadelphia, right? I got to teach her to live in America.

- How do you begin a discussion with your child about his race and culture?

- How do you talk about race without making your child bitter?

Given our belief that racism is alive and well in American society, that Black youth and families are negatively targeted and isolated, and that many Whites may misinterpret Black behavior, we feel that African American children need a keen historical and contemporary understanding of their cultural distinctiveness. This something extra is what we talked about briefly in Chapter One—cultural pride reinforcement, or CPR.

"Missed, Dissed, and Pissed"

The misinterpretation of Black behavior by Whites is a constant fear of Black parents. One reason to apply correction is that Whites may exaggerate the nature of common, everyday Black cultural style. If a Black youth is being "cool," it may be seen as being "defiant." If she is being bright and eager to express herself, she may be seen as being "rude, boisterous, and aggressive." We think that Black youth are often "missed, dissed, and pissed." That is, they are misinterpreted as problematic when they are not, disrespected because their normal, culturally unique styles of adolescence are perceived as adultlike or criminal, and they are angry about being subject to misinterpretation and disrespect.

But there has to be more to parenting adolescents than survival training. All of us need help to teach our children how to "make it" in this world. African Americans need to focus on protection, affection, and correction strategies not only because we are a targeted and isolated people but also because of our cultural distinctiveness. We must understand and promote this culture in order for African American youth to make sense of their racial identities and manage the anger that flows from being misunderstood on such a grand scale.

Cultural Pride Reinforcement Is About Self-Actualization

Although *survival* is essential, it is not sufficient. We also need our children to *grow* and creatively use their God-given talents and access their cultural center, whatever that center is. In other words, healthy children of color become so by stretching themselves. Wade Nobles (1991), a noted African American social psychologist, identifies two enduring characteristics of African cultures around the world: "survival of the tribe" and "oneness of being." Survival is about how Black folk have endured enormous oppression and how we may have to endure struggles indefinitely. Oneness represents a unique ability to be in harmony with one's environment and the nature and people that inhabit it. It also represents the hope that we can get along with and care for each other, especially our children.

CPR is a process Black parents can use to remind children that their difference is an asset, not a liability. We feel that the lives of Black youth are at risk as long as fearful authority figures like police misinterpret their cultural style as hostility or aggression. Therefore knowledge to combat this consistent misinterpretation can help to save their lives. CPR cannot be given enough and will take many forms in interactions and messages. In a world that rejects difference, CPR is essential to counteracting the fears, projections, and violence of a racist society. CPR also involves teaching children about the insecurities of the world, what to expect from others who cannot rid themselves of the negative effects of racism, and how to defend themselves in the event that they are confronted with this racism in blatant and subtle forms.

Being Both Proactive and Protective

There is a need for racial socialization in Black families that includes both proactive and protective messages. Too much of the "Watch out for those who will misinterpret you" message without the "Be proud of who you are and where you came from" message can be challenging to young souls and spirits that need to be creative and dream as well as be wary and vigilant. All three authors have conducted research regarding the psychological benefits of active communication with African American children and youth. In fact, our findings indicate that only half of Black families directly discuss racism and how to deal with it. We propose that racial socialization is an important facet of a discipline strategy.

The role of resisting societal oppression as a cultural value in African American communities is not restricted to adult behavior but involves children as well. We pay special attention to the heritage of storytelling among African American families. Cultural storytelling is one of the ways Black parents teach their children to endure racial hostility and develop racial pride as they live in a world that is prejudiced against them. Preteenhood is when they start to need the information and begin to apply the lessons from those stories. Research demonstrates that this racial storytelling, or racial socialization, is essential to the psychological health of African Americans.

∽

Nothing wipes your tears away but your own hand.

∽

Howard Stevenson's research has identified two major types of messages that parents use to communicate to their children about culture, race, racism, and race relations. One way parents talk to their children about race and racism is *protective*, and the other is *proactive*. Protective parenting about race and culture involves messages and interactions with children about how to survive life by dealing with racial oppression. These messages include "You have to work twice as hard as the next person to get ahead because you are Black." Another example is "Don't talk back to police, and don't run from them. They don't know you to be the sweet, adorable child that I know you to be. Some police officers think you are going to hurt them. Be polite and respectful." Proactive cultural transmission messages and interactions communicate to children how to self-actualize by appreciating and embracing the creative and healing aspects of their cultural heritage, without worrying as much about oppression or what Whites or others think about Blacks.

Protective Racial Messages Parents Say to Their Preteens

1. "If you get stopped by police, don't resist. And whatever you do, don't run."

2. "If police or authority figures stop you, don't curse at them. And do what they tell you."

3. "If police or authority figures speak to you, speak to them nicely and say, 'Yes, sir' and 'No, sir.'"

4. "Be careful of staring down other people because they may think you want to fight."

5. "If your teacher accuses you of wrongdoing, ask her in a polite manner to explain herself."

6. "When teachers and police officers are ignorant of our culture and tend to consider us animals or criminals, you must be smarter than they are by not inciting their basest fears."

We believe that discipline must be understood within both protective and proactive racial socialization orientations because to discipline from a perspective of protection alone will often leave us desperate to "save children from a hostile world" and lead us to underemphasize their need for nurturance. To communicate only proactive racial messages may help the child to understand his or her potential in the world while appreciating his cultural or bicultural heritage but may not prepare the child psychologically for racial oppression, should it occur. We believe that parents need to think about discipline from both protective (resistance-to-oppression focus) and proactive (promotion-of-cultural-empowerment focus) orientations in order for our children to grow healthy, wealthy, and wise. So we believe that understanding discipline in a cultural context makes it more effective than if it is understood as an isolated event like spanking.

Emotional Martial Arts

As children reach preadolescence, the stakes are higher. We have to teach our young boys and girls more concrete strategies. If Black youth are targeted as problems, then why wouldn't we tell them how to defend themselves without getting killed?

Proactive Racial Messages Parents Say to Their Preteens

1. "When people tell you that you aren't smart enough, remember Malcolm and Martin."

2. "Be yourself, or you will be by yourself."

3. "God may not always come when you call Him, but He's always right on time."

4. "Only what you do for Christ [or Allah] will last."

5. "The greatest love of all is inside of me."

6. "Who are my people, and what is my history?"

7. "Not every White person is racist. And racists are not bad people, just scared people. This still makes them dangerous. So look on them as helpless rather than powerful and take your power from your family, your culture, your people, and your God, not from them."

All three authors direct a program called Cultural Pride Reinforcement (CPR) for African American Boys with the goal of teaching boys with troubled histories of aggression how to manage their anger and how to stay away from danger. We define danger in a number of ways. The most important danger is a lack of self-knowledge. If you don't know where you came from, who you are, or who your people are, you will never have a meaningful future to speak of. Although many have experiences of being falsely accused, harassed, or beaten by police, being followed by store clerks, and being at risk of getting shot or injured from living in violent neighborhoods, few of them have a clue that being Black has anything to do with these things—until we explain it. We tell them because we think their lives depend on it. And for many, it starts to sink in. Amazingly, we argue back and forth, but in the end they listen.

CPR is emotional martial arts. Like other self-defense systems, its goal is to help the child understand his or her individual *and* collective self. Like other martial arts, CPR helps folks defend themselves through self-knowledge rather than out of fear or self-ignorance. Ironically, parents need and can learn the emotional self-defense strategies of CPR too. CPR teaches our children and us to be proud of our differences and to embrace them, even if they are defined as weaknesses by others. This is so important a message to preadolescents who are in the throes of developing an identity and asking tough identity questions. You can't build a self on something you are not, so you might as well start with what God gave you. And that includes the "good" and the "not so good." You may never know fully why God gives you particular assets and liabilities until later on in life. So don't reject your self before you know who your self is. Why? Because "what goes around comes around."

Who Are My People, and to Whom Do I Belong?

Now, when we use the word *self*, we are not talking about the "me, myself, and I." We mean the "me, you, and us"—the collective self. In our view preadolescents can be more protected if they are told that none of us can claim to have reached our current station in life without some help from others. In CPR we seek to challenge the rugged individualism that pervades our schools, our workplaces, and our relationships. We try to help families face and deal with the personal and racial identity struggle. Personal identity development tries to answer the question, "Who am I, and who will I be?" Racial identity development tries to answer the question, "Who are my people, and to whom do I belong?" African Americans must maintain and rekindle a sense of our cultural and collective unity and uniqueness as each defines his or her own personal and racial identity. We must help our children to ponder, "Who are my people?" This is what Gary and Sheila (in Chapter Four) are stumbling to help their son, Ahmad, learn—step by painful step. If they don't give up, it can be a wonderful lesson to learn.

John Henrick Clarke, an African historian, makes a distinction between Western culture's model of the *individual* self and the African model of the *collective* self. He suggests that the individual definition of self follows from Descartes's old principle that "I think, therefore I am." In contrast, the African collective definition of self follows from the principle that "I am because we are, and we are because I am." These are two very different ways to think about self and existence. However, personal identity ("I am") need not get lost through the search for one's collective identity ("We are").

The teenage boys in the CPR group boast about everything. They can jump higher, get more girls, and outsmart anyone. When we confront them about the limits of their ability to influence the world, none concede. Then we remind them of the history of enslavement and the statistics of Black male life in America and ask them to tell us about some of their male relatives who also had big egos and ended up dead or in jail. We can also show them that they belong to a glorious family and history and that some have successfully managed oppression without such negative outcomes. But they have to learn how to keep their egos in check and realize how people react to them just because they are Black.

When children can see themselves as part of the collective, then they can *be* less afraid of the hostility that they are faced with, wherever it may come from. Parents can also feel less afraid of the hostility in the midst of which they are raising their children. In addition, both African American parents and children can begin to develop personal and racial identities that do not rely on oppression or hostility but on pride in self and each other. To *be* somebody, in the collective sense, is to *be*long to a larger network of relationships that watch over, give lots of affection, and hold one accountable for one's behavior. Being and existing are not based on just what I am or become but also on what "I in relationship to us" am and become. This is what Nobles (1991) means by "oneness of being."

In a Western cultural model, we often get to know people by asking, "What do you do?" instead of "To whom do you belong?" The former question often leads us to describe ourselves by telling folks what we have accomplished, where we work, or what school we went to—things. "To whom do you belong?" is a question about being as defined by relationships. We believe that African American parenting and discipline must move away from the development of "human doings" and toward the development of "human beings."

In addition to teaching emotional awareness of the collective self and defending from the larger hostility, CPR can help youth interpret the world more accurately. African American child rearing needs CPR to help children and families make sense of this confused hostility and prevent children from blaming themselves for that hostility. They can learn when to care and be vulnerable rather than to strike first and ask questions later. They can learn to appreciate their anger as a part of life and a signal for reflection and expression, not a trigger for aggression.

Perhaps an analogy may help. It is not hard for most to understand how a child may blame him- or herself for sexual or physical abuse even though the child was victimized. Without feedback, this trauma can burden the child to explain it using him- or herself as the responsible party. The same is true in racial trauma or any trauma. Without intervention, recipients of abuse will internalize the pain. CPR says that children are not responsible for racial hostility and can learn over time to reject all of its negative psychological impacts. African American children can make choices about how they want to define their racial selves.

"Because We Said So"

CPR is important when we are supervising our children and teenagers, when we are giving them hugs and kisses, and when they are doing wrong. Amazingly, when we apply CPR in this way, children will eventually learn to protect themselves, love themselves, and correct themselves. Youth who know themselves, their culture, and the meaning behind the world's hostility can navigate through the world with a map, making meaningful choices—which is really all most parents really want. We want our children to learn how to make meaningful choices about themselves and others. There is a proverb that goes, "To one who does not know, a small garden is a forest." When our children are unaware of their histories, their culture, their families, their environment, themselves, they are at risk of steering their lives without direction and without confidence.

So we must teach them CPR every day with our words *and* our actions. As children develop emotional martial arts, they can make choices about what and whom to trust and can bond appropriately. These little CPR interactions may not seem like much, but they are vital to our children's survival *and* growth.

One of the boys asks CPR teacher Hassan about "driving while Black." What did he mean by that? And Brother Hassan, who was teaching CPR that day, explained that it was the unwritten policy and practice of the New Jersey state police to arrest Black motorists on the turnpike because they believed Blacks were natural criminals, even if there was no legal reason to stop them. They were all surprised. The idea of racism as a planned strategy was a shock to them. They knew White police officers could be mean sometimes, but they didn't comprehend it as a conspiracy or part of their job. We couldn't wait to tell them how to deal with this kind of injustice. They couldn't wait to listen.

If Gary and Sheila (from Chapter Four) consider that they are not alone in trying to keep their son alive, healthy, and proud to be an African American, they can save themselves a lot of stress. Black *is* beautiful, but in order to make that more than a slogan as their son moves into adolescence, they will need a posse, a village, and a lot of prayer.

Venus and Serena Williams, the professional tennis phenoms, have taken the world by storm, not only by their unprecedented tennis talent, power, and style but by their flair off the court. Two of the most exciting moments in sports history were watching Serena win the U.S. Open and seeing Venus win Wimbledon—both of them representing African American people with a sense of joy and vibrancy. The media hype about these teenagers being African Americans, about their father being a rogue tennis coach who shielded them from the spotlight early (much to the chagrin of tennis commentators and legends), and about their raw power—a racist feeding frenzy—was painful to watch. The failure of predominantly White sports reporters, journalists, and commentators to identify the talent of these two teens, to appreciate their embrace of cultural heritage and identity, and to avoid trashing their methods of learning tennis was evident once these two won a Grand Slam Tournament.

It is always painful for us as African Americans to watch how the media consistently miss the deeper meanings and issues that matter to Black folk. But it feels violent when the media attack in ways that go beyond the meaning of sports or journalism, seemingly for the sake of sensationalism. It was equally wonderful to watch the teens' girlish responses when they won the tournaments, something that seems to be missing from the sport of tennis and most sports for that matter. The consistent pressure placed on young children to become adults and lose some of their childhood emotional expressions has plagued professional tennis. Venus and Serena were as joyous as you would expect teenage girls to be, and that was another "I told you so" that many African Americans (tennis lovers and non–tennis lovers alike) voiced to the world and particularly to the media, which consistently failed to appreciate them.

Well, in an interview for the magazine *Elle* (Friedman, 2000), Serena was asked if she was tired of being considered a *Black* tennis star instead of just a tennis star. After challenging the intent of the question of the interviewer, she retorted that she was proud to be a Black tennis star and to be Black because so many children looked up to her for that. This showed that she understood the deeper-level dynamics of race in our world and that the interviewer's attempts to create controversy were ignorant of the possibility that Blackness is good. It appeared to us that Serena and Venus's parents had taught them how to appreciate their cultural identities, to identify the insidious and subtle nature of racism, and yet to be developmentally appropriate as children, then teenagers, in their cultural expression.

As teachers in the CPR group, we all consider ourselves "parents" to these future young men. Whereas the world sees them as a "menace to society," we see them as our "children" and consider it our responsibility to simultaneously warn and encourage them. The world is small, and we belong to each other. If we don't begin to use protection, affection, and correction for tomorrow's children, they will have no reason to take care of themselves, their families, and their community.

References

American Academy of Pediatrics, Committee on Psychosocial Aspects of Child and Family Health. "Guidance for Effective Discipline." *Pediatrics*, 1998, *101*, 723–728.

Baumrind, D. "An Exploratory Study of Socialization Effects on Black Children: Some Black-White Comparisons." *Child Development*, 1972, *43*, 261–267.

Edelman, M. W. *Disproportionate Minority Confinement*. Washington, D.C.: Children's Defense Fund, 2000.

Fanon, F. *Black Skin, White Masks*. New York: Grove, 1962.

Ferebee, J. *Got It Goin' On: Fitness and Fashion with Funk*. Washington, D.C.: Got It Goin' On Publications, 1996.

Friedman, D. "Sister Act." *Elle*, Jan. 2000, pp. 93–105.

Majors, R., and Billson, J. M. *Cool Pose: The Dilemmas of Black Manhood in America*. New York: Lexington Books, 1992.

Marley, B. *Redemption Song*. Produced by Bob Marley and the Wailers, Bob Marley Music, Inc., Kingston, Jamaica, 1980.

Nobles, W. "African Philosophy: Foundations for Black Psychology." In R. L. Jones (ed.), *Black Psychology*. Hampton, Va.: Cobb & Henry, 1991.

Pinderhughes, E. E., and others. "Discipline Responses: Influences of Parents' Socioeconomic Status, Ethnicity, Beliefs About Parenting, Stress, and Cognitive-Emotional Processes." *Journal of Family Psychology*, 2000, *14*, 380–400.

Romer, D., Jamieson, K. H., and de Coteau, N. J. "The Treatment of Persons of Color in Local Television News: Ethnic Blame Discourse or Realistic Group Conflict?" *Communication Research*, 1998, *25*, 286–305.

Snyder, H. N., and Sickmund, M. *Juvenile Offenders and Victims: 1999 National Report*. Washington, D.C.: Office of Juvenile Justice and Delinquency Prevention, 1999.

Spencer, M. B., Cunningham, M., and Swanson, D. P. "Identity as Coping: Adolescent African-American Males' Adaptive Responses to High-Risk Environment." In H. W. Harris and others (eds.), *Racial and Ethnic Identity: Psychological Development and Creative Expression*. New York: Routledge, 1995.

Stanlaw, J., and Peshkin, A. "Black Invisibility in a Multiethnic High School." In L. Weis (ed.), *Class, Race, and Gender in U.S. Schools*. Albany, N.Y.: SUNY Press, 1988.

Stevenson, H. C. "Raising Safe Villages: Cultural-Ecological Factors That Influence the Emotional Adjustment of Adolescents." *Journal of Black Psychology*, 1998a, *24*, 44–59.

Stevenson, H. C. "The Confluence of the 'Both-And' in Racial Identity Theory." In R. Jones (ed.), *African American Identity Development: Theory, Research, and Intervention*. Hampton, Va.: Cobb & Henry, 1998b.

Ward, J. V. "Raising Resisters: The Role of Truth Telling in the Psychological Development of African American Girls." In B. J. Leadbeater and others (eds.), *Urban Girls: Resisting Stereotypes, Creating Identities*. New York: New York University Press, 1996.

Watts, R. J., and Abdul-Adil, J. K. "Promoting Critical Consciousness in Young, African-American Men." *Journal of Prevention & Intervention in the Community*, 1997, *16*, 63–86.

West, C. *Race Matters*. Boston: Beacon Press, 1993.

Wilson, A. N. *Black-on-Black Violence: The Psychodynamics of Black Self-Annihilation in Service of White Domination*. Bronx, N.Y.: African World InfoSystems, 1990.

Wright, M. *I'm Chocolate, You're Vanilla: Raising Healthy Black and Biracial Children in a Race-Conscious World: A Guide for Parents and Teachers*. San Francisco: Jossey-Bass, 1998.

Resources for Child Rearing and Discipline

Organization and Web Site	Purpose and Constituency
Infancy Through Elementary School Age	
AllAboutParents.com http://www.allaboutparents. com	Offers information on pregnancy and birth, healthy living, caring for babies and toddlers, work and money, shopping, and other issues; focuses on parents of babies and toddlers
Baby's Story http://www.babysstory.com Leaning Post Productions 487 Hulsetown Rd. Campbell Hall, NY 10916 845-496-4709	Offers illustrated journal pages and e-cards that parents can use to record, print, save, and e-mail memorable events in the lives of their babies from before birth through age six
Earlychildhood.com http://www.earlychildhood. com	Provides ideas and advice for all new parents
FamilyPlay http://www.familyplay.com	Provides parents with kid's activities, daily bedtime stories, child-rearing advice, and reviews of children's Web sites

Sesame Workshop
http://www.sesameworkshop.
  org

Offers activities and advice
for parent and baby

urbanbaby.com
http://www.urbanbaby.com

On-line resource for urban
parents; features advice on
pregnancy, baby gear, clothing,
health, kid-friendly travel,
and events

Preadolescents and Adolescents

Adolescence Directory
  On-Line
http://education.indiana.
edu/cas/adol/adol.html

A service of the Center for
Adolescent Studies at Indiana
University that provides
information on adolescent issues
(such as conflict, violence, and
physical and mental health
issues) for educators, counselors,
parents, researchers, health
practitioners, and teens

Do Right Foundation
http://www.doright.org
852 5th Ave., Suite 215
San Diego, CA 92101

Seeks to fund pilot programs
addressing violence prevention,
joblessness, justice system
productivity, welfare,
government efficiency, and
parenting skills

Greater Washington Urban
League Parent Center
http://www.gwulparentcenter.
  org
3501 14th St. NW
Washington, D.C. 20010
202-265-8200

Offers parenting tips and
information on student
achievement, colleges,
and scholarships

All Ages

African American Child http://www.aachild.com	Includes resources, news, and shopping links specific to the African American community
Alpha Pregnancy Care Center http://www.alphacare.org 11 Herbert Dr. Latham, NY 12110 518-785-6525	Provides in New York state counseling for women dealing with pregnancy issues, instruction in parenting skills and CPR, and job training
Anderson School at UCLA http://www.anderson.ucla.edu 110 Westwood Plaza Box 951481 Los Angeles, CA 90095-1481 310-825-6121	Offers training in managerial skills for directors, board members, and other key personnel of child-care agencies
Black Parenting Website http://www.blackparenting. com	Web site of the *Black Parenting Book,* which focuses on the first five years of a child's life; offers the opportunity to read book excerpts, ask the authors questions, and discuss issues with Black parents; provides information on children's health and development as well as advice reflecting cultural realities to help parents start their children out in life with a sense of heritage, self-esteem, and racial pride

Black Student Fund
http://www.blackstudentfund.
 org
3636 16th St. NW, 4th Floor
Washington, D.C. 20010-1146
202-387-1414

Provides financial assistance and support services to Washington, D.C., metropolitan area African American students, grades pre-kindergarten through 12, and their families, and financial assistance and support services that reach thousands in both the greater Washington, D.C., area and the nation; offers parents information on options for educating their children; provides multiracial training to teachers; networks Black educators into the independent school system

Bridge to Understanding
http://www.bridgeto
 understanding.com

Offers an on-line journal and directory of resources for professionals and all parents concerned with young people not meeting expectations

Circle Association
http://www.math.buffalo.
 edu/~sww/circle/circle.html

Provides information on the Circle Association, a group of African American men dedicated to promoting and improving quality of life, parenting skills, economic growth and development, and the pursuit of excellence and spiritual development of African Americans

Common Sense Parenting
http://www.parenting.org

Answers parents' questions
about parenting and provides
resources for better parenting

Connect for Kids
http://www.connectforkids.org
Benton Foundation
950 18th St. NW
Washington, D.C. 20006

Provides information and
resources for adults who want
to make their communities
work for kids

DrSpock.com
http://www.drspock.com

Provides news, original articles,
and answers to parents' questions
in a community environment

ERIC Clearinghouse on
  Urban Education
http://eric-web.tc.columbia.edu
Institute for Urban and
  Minority Education
Teachers College, Box 40
Columbia University
New York, NY 10027
800-601-4868

Provides access to research-
based information about the
process of parenting and
about family involvement
in education

Las Madres Neighborhood
  Playgroups
http://www.lasmadres.org
408-265-4056

Offers parents opportunities
for friendship, support, and new
things to do; offers children the
chance to learn socialization
skills

Learning Seed
http://learningseed.com
330 Telser Rd.
Lake Zurich, IL 60047
800-634-4941

Sells educational videos and
software on nutrition, consumers
education, parenting, critical
thinking, and other topics

National Parent Information Network http://npin.org University of Illinois at Urbana-Champaign Children's Research Center 51 Gerty Dr. Champaign, IL 61820-7469 217-333-1386 or 800-583-4135	Provides access to research-based information about the process of parenting and about family involvement in education
National Parenting Center http://www.tnpc.com 800-753-6667	Provides parents information on raising children, from pregnancy and birth through adolescence
National PTA http://www.pta.org 330 N. Wabash Ave., Suite 2100 Chicago, IL 60611 312-670-6782 or 800-307-4PTA (4782)	Promotes the education, health, and safety of children and families; has offices in every state
"On the Wings of Love . . ."— Dealing with Difficult Children http://gswt01.tripod.com	Offers insights for parents dealing with children's behavioral disorders; includes a message board, chat, and links
Parent Soup http://www.parentsoup.com	Offers parents the opportunity to discuss and learn about parenting, kids, adoption, family issues, dating, money, travel, entertainment, and other issues; includes input from experts and others

Parenting.com http://www.parenting. com/parenting	Contains articles, tips, and discussions on all aspects of pregnancy and raising a child
Parents Edge http://www.parentsedge.com	Offers educational and family resources with advice on child development, homework, skills building, and Internet learning games for children
ParentsAssociation.com http://www.parentsassociation. com	Provides a forum for parents of children, adolescents, and college-age young adults
Parents.com http://www.parents.com	Offers information from Parents Magazine
Parentsroom http://www.parentsroom.org	Offers the opportunity to post questions and responses about parenting issues and options
parenttalksurvey.com http://www.parenttalksurvey. com	Offers the opportunity to participate in a study about strengthening parent-child communication
Peace & Harmony Un-Ltd. http://home.earthlink.net/ ~harmonyunltd	Provides child-rearing advice, through questions to a child-care expert, for parents wishing to enhance their parenting skills
Positive Discipline http://www.positivediscipline. com	Offers workshops, parenting classes, products, and articles for parents, teachers, counselors,

Empowering People, Inc.
P.O. Box 1926
Orem, UT 84059-1926
800-456-7770

nurses, and pediatricians; allows parents to ask questions; social workers who work with and care for young people

Score! Parenting Game
http://www1.kaplan.com/
   view/games/ga_scoreqa/
   intro/navless

Offers parents a game to test their parenting skills

Scratch Back Club
http://www.geocities.com/
   sbcjune93
1488 Queen St. W, #90037
Toronto, Ontario M6K 1L0
Canada

Provides opportunities to forge mutual aid alliances and increase Afrocentric awareness for one-parent families of Black children and two-parent families in which there are multiracial African children (not limited to Canadian families)

Single African American
   Fathers' Exchange
http://www.saafe.com

Provides services and information on parenting for single African American fathers

TeachParents.Com
http://www.teachparents.com
National Parenting Institute
P.O. Box 1252
Temecula, CA 92593
909-694-8910

Offers a self-study course from the National Parenting Institute to improve parenting skills or meet court- or agency-mandated parenting course requirements

Wing of Madness Depression
   Community
http://www.wingofmadness.com

Provides information on clinical depression in children

workfamilytips.com	Offers parents the opportunity
http://www.workfamilytips.com	to share quick, helpful tips on
	balancing work and family

Worldview Publishing, Inc.	Produces videos on conflict
http://www.worldviewpub.com	resolution, social skills, and
521 Herchel Dr.	discipline training for preteens,
Tampa, FL 33617	teenagers, and parents
800-987-9444	

Texts on Discipline

Bailey, B. A. *Easy to Love, Difficult to Discipline: The Seven Basic Skills for Turning Conflict into Cooperation*. New York: Morrow, 2000.

Bloomquist, M. L. *Skills Training for Children with Behavior Disorders: A Parent and Therapist Guidebook*. New York: Guilford Press, 1996.

Bodenhamer, G. *Parent in Control: Restore Order in Your Home and Create a Loving Relationship with Your Adolescent*. New York: Simon & Schuster, 1995.

Canter, L., and Canter, M. *Assertive Discipline for Parents: A Proven Step-by-Step Approach to Solving Everyday Behavior Problems*. New York: HarperCollins, 1993.

Coloroso, B. *Kids Are Worth It! Giving Your Child the Gift of Inner Discipline*. New York: Morrow, 1995.

Curwin, R. L., and Mendler, A. N. *Discipline with Dignity*. Alexandria, Va.: Association for Supervision and Curriculum Development, 1999.

Henner, M., and Sharon, R. V. *I Refuse to Raise a Brat: Straightforward Advice on Parenting in an Age of Overindulgence*. New York: Regan Books, 2000.

Leman, K. *Making Children Mind Without Losing Yours*. Grand Rapids, Mich.: Chosen Books, 2000.

Mackenzie, R. J. *Setting Limits: How to Raise Responsible, Independent Children by Providing Clear Boundaries*. Roseville, Calif.: Prima, 1998.

Nelson, J., Glenn, H. S., and Lott, L. *Positive Discipline A-Z: From Toddlers to Teens—1001 Solutions to Everyday Parenting Problems*. Roseville, Calif.: Prima, 1999.

Ricker, A., and Crowder, C. *Backtalk: Four Steps to Ending Rude Behavior in Your Kids*. New York: Simon & Schuster, 1998.

Ricker, A., and Crowder, C. *Whining: 3 Steps to Stopping It Before the Tears and Tantrums Start*. New York: Simon & Schuster, 2000.

Samalin, N., and Jablow, M. M. *Loving Your Child Is Not Enough: Positive Discipline That Works*. New York: Viking Penguin, 1998.

Sears, W., and Sears, M. *The Discipline Book: Everything You Need to Know to Have a Better-Behaved Child—from Birth to Age Ten*. Vol. 1. New York: Little, Brown, 1995.

Wyckoff, J., and Unell, B. *Discipline Without Shouting or Spanking: Practical Solutions to the Most Common Preschool Behavior Problems*. Minnetonka, Minn.: Meadowbrook Press, 1984.

York, D., and Wachtel, T. *Toughlove*. New York: Bantam Books, 1983.

Texts on African American Parenting

Alvy, K. T. *Black Parenting: Strategies for Training*. New York: Irvington, 1992.

Barnes, A. S. *Single Parents in Black America: A Study in Culture and Legitimacy*. Bristol, Ind.: Wyndham Hall Press, 1987.

Barras, J. R. *Whatever Happened to Daddy's Little Girl? The Impact of Fatherlessness on Black Women*. New York: Random House, 2000.

Beal, A. C., Villarosa, L., and Abner, A. *The Black Parenting Book: Caring for Our Children in the First Five Years*. New York: Broadway Books, 1998.

Bernstine, A. C. *As for Me and My House: Some Redemptive Words for the Black Family*. West Berlin, N.J.: Townsend Press, 1993.

Black, C. *It's Never Too Late to Have a Happy Childhood: Inspirations for Adult Children*. New York: Random House, 1989.

Black, D. A. *The Myth of Adolescence: Raising Responsible Children in an Irresponsible Society*. Santa Ana, Calif.: Davidson Press, 1999.

Black, T., and Stephenson, L. R. *Kicking Your Kids out of the Nest: Raising Your Children for Life on Their Own*. Grand Rapids, Mich.: Zondervan, 1995.

Bowser, B. R. *Black Male Adolescents: Parenting and Education in Community Context*. Lanham, Md.: University Press of America, 1994.

Breggie, J., Black, C., and Harris, A. *Beyond Our Mothers' Footsteps*. Alpharetta, Ga.: Beejay Enterprises, 1998.

Brown, K. M., and Cowans, A. W. *Sacred Bond: Black Men and Their Mothers*. New York: Little, Brown, 2000.

Bush, L. *Can Black Mothers Raise Our Sons?* Chicago: African American Images, 1999.

Children's Defense Fund. *Black Community Crusade and Covenant for Protecting Children*. Washington, D.C.: Children's Defense Fund, 1995.

Comer, J. P., and Poussaint, A. F. *Raising Black Children: Two Leading Psychiatrists Confront the Educational, Social, and Emotional Problems Facing Black Children*. New York: Plume, 1992.

Copage, E. V. *Black Pearls for Parents: Meditations, Affirmations, and Inspirations for African American Parents*. New York: Morrow, 1995.

Enns, G., and Black, J. *It's Not Okay Anymore: Your Personal Guide to Ending Abuse, Taking Charge, and Loving Yourself*. Oakland, Calif.: New Harbinger, 1997.

Golden, M. *Saving Our Sons: Raising Black Children in a Turbulent World*. New York: Doubleday, 1995.

Harris, F. *In The Black: The African American Parent's Guide to Raising Financially Responsible Children*. New York: Simon & Schuster, 1999.

Harris, P. *From the Soul of the Black Family: Stories of Great Black Parents and the Lives They Gave Us*. New York: Putnam, forthcoming.

Hopson, D. P., and Powell-Hopson, D. S. *Different and Wonderful: Raising Black Children in a Race-Conscious Society*. Upper Saddle River, N.J.: Prentice Hall, 1991.

Hutchinson, E. O. *Black Fatherhood: The Guide to Male Parenting*. Los Angeles: Middle Passage Press, 1992.

Hutchinson, E. O. *Black Fatherhood II: Black Women Talk About Their Men*. Los Angeles: Middle Passage Press, 1994.

Jackson, V. *Racism and Child Protection: The Black Experience of Child Sexual Abuse*. New York: Continuum, 1996.

Kafele, B. K. *Black Parents' Handbook to Educating Your Children: Outside of the Classroom*. Jersey City, N.J.: Baruti, 1999.

Kunjufu, J. *Developing Positive Self-Imaging and Discipline in Black Children*. Chicago: African American Images, 1985.

McLaughlin, C. J., Frisby, D. R., and Williams, M. W. *The Black Parents' Handbook: A Guide to Healthy Pregnancy, Birth, and Child Care*. Orlando, Fla.: Harcourt Brace, 1990.

Moore, P. A. *How Not to Abuse Your Child: Written by a Black Mother Who "Spared the Rod" and Successfully Raised Eleven Youngsters—Ten of Whom Are Boys*. Detroit, Mich.: Detroit Black Writer's Guild, 1985.

Patterson, C., Strickland, A. E., and Perchinske, M. *Commitment: Fatherhood in Black America*. St. Louis: University of Missouri Press, 1998.

Perkins, U. E. *Harvesting New Generations: The Positive Development of Black Youth*. Chicago: Third World Press, 1998.

Porter, J. D. *Black Child, White Child: The Development of Racial Attitudes*. Cambridge, Mass.: Harvard University Press, 1971.

Puckett, M. B., and Black, J. K. *The Young Child: Development from Prebirth Through Age Eight*. Upper Saddle River, N.J.: Prentice Hall, 1995.

Smith, W. C. *The Church in the Life of the Black Family*. Valley Forge, Pa.: Judson Press, 1995.

Wilson, A. N. *Developmental Psychology of the Black Child*. New York: Africana Research, 1978.

Wilson, A. N. *Awakening the Natural Genius of Black Children*. New York: African World Infosystems, 1993.

Wright, M. A. *I'm Chocolate, You're Vanilla: Raising Healthy Black and Biracial Children in a Race-Conscious World: A Guide for Parents and Teachers*. San Francisco: Jossey-Bass, 2000.

The Authors

HOWARD C. STEVENSON is a father of a ten-year-old and is a tenured associate professor of education in the School, Community, and Child Clinical Psychology Program in the Graduate School of Education, Psychology in Education Division, at the University of Pennsylvania. Stevenson's clinical and academic efforts have been directed toward identifying and mobilizing cultural strengths in African American families to improve the psychological adjustment of children and adolescents. He has coauthored several articles related to the impact of culture on the psychological functioning of African Americans and other minorities. He is also a consultant for community-based organizations on cultural issues in child and family mental health. He has been invited to provide keynote speeches to audiences as diverse as presidential task force social scientists and local gatherings of urban and rural Head Start parents. He holds a faculty appointment in the Center for Research in Evaluation and Social Policy and in the Interdisciplinary Studies in Human Development Program, both housed in the Psychology in Education Division at the University of Pennsylvania. Stevenson obtained a doctorate in clinical psychology at Fuller Graduate School of Psychology and a master's degree in theology from Fuller Theological Seminary, both in 1985. Stevenson has twelve years of unique experience as a clinical supervisor in community and school consultation and family and child psychotherapy.

GWENDOLYN DAVIS received her master's degree in social work in 1989 and her doctorate in 1999 in the School, Community, and Child Clinical Psychology Program, both from the University of Pennsylvania. She has several years of experience as a research coordinator of community action research intervention projects in school and community center settings and has worked with children and families for over fifteen years. Davis has expertise as a therapist, as a case manager for multiproblem families and prisoners, and as a child advocate in the Defender Association of Philadelphia. She understands well the complexity of helping systems and how adolescents and children are too often without help in addressing the violence that they experience as well as the violence to which they are exposed. A social worker and psychologist, Davis has a wealth of knowledge about the negative effects of abusive parenting on children and how that contributes to aggressive behavior.

SABURAH ABDUL-KABIR serves as the community research coordinator of the Community Outreach Through Parent Empowerment project at the University of Pennsylvania. She has ten years of experience as a community coordinator and consultant on funded projects serving urban low-income families. She has served as a panelist on research forums in early childhood and is known for her wisdom and competence regarding raising Black children in a racially hostile world. She has given presentations on parenting issues at several childhood intervention conferences. She has received several awards from national organizations for her outstanding professional and volunteer services. Abdul-Kabir is an expert regarding the role of spirituality and religion in child rearing and discipline. She has a lifetime of personal experience as a wife and a mother of six children.

Index

A

Abdul-Adil, J., 156

Abdul-Kabir, S., 58

Absent parent, submerged anger at, 122

Accountability: and caring, 12; and correction, 11–14; and cycle of rejection, 120; *versus* punishment, 12–13

Acting out, 96

Adolescence: character in, 145–147; combating catch-33 in, 160–162; countering cool in, 155–157; and dealing with the system, 163–165; hypervulnerability in, 153–155, 157; individual cool in, 151–153; and meaning of life, 145; and mental slavery, 162–163; need for independence in, 144–145; self-discipline in, 143–181; social image in, 148–149; and understanding blackness, 150–151; and understanding systemic nature of catch-33, 158–160

Affection: as children become social beings, 82–83; definition of, 7; in elementary school-age children, 81–88; and emotional nurturing, 86–88; in infant and toddler stage, 56–63; as key ingredient to discipline, 5–7; in preadolescence,

118–127; results of, 112–113; and spoiling, 85–88; understanding how Black youth may not be nurtured by others in, 82–83

Africa: and African proverbs, 6, 12, 79, 108, 169, 178; and African psychology, 56, 108, 171; and African religious philosophy, 19, 26, 39

African American children: improving psychological future of, 21; margin of error for, 90; perceiving, as gifts, 67; projection of anger on, 48; victimization of, 8

African American parents: and both-and parenting, 37–42; effect of racism on, 16–18; and need for special book on discipline, 14–21; special fears for, 62

Agassi, A., 148

Ageism, 149–150

Aggression, 8

Alcohol abuse, 148

American Academy of Pediatrics, 15

Anger: and hypertension, 72; in infant and toddler stages, 68–69; projection of, on children, 48; as result of frustration, 36; as result of punishment, 13; as signal for reflection, 178; and spanking, 108; submerged, at absent parent, 122

Animalistic imagery, 90